DARE TO
BREAK
THE MOULD

*For Linda,
Charlotte and Olivia,
my family of mould-breakers*

DARE TO BREAK THE MOULD

Making sense of
the Bible • worship • doubt
guidance
spiritual warfare

Simon Jones

frameworks

FRAMEWORKS
38 De Montfort Street, Leicester LE1 7GP, England

© Simon Jones, 1993

First published 1993

British Library Cataloguing in Publication Data
A catalogue record for this book is available from
the British Library.

ISBN 0–85111–221–8

**Phototypeset in Great Britain by Intype, London
Printed and bound in Great Britain by
Cox & Wyman Ltd, Reading, Berkshire**

*Frameworks is an imprint of Inter-Varsity Press, the
book-publishing division of the Universities and Colleges
Christian Fellowship.*

CONTENTS

Foreword by Steve Chalke 7

Introduction: Breaking the mould 9

1. Opening the book 13

2. Getting to know you 31

3. Once more, with feeling 45

4. There are more questions than answers 61

5. I don't know which way to turn 77

6. Whatever happened to the world and the flesh? 91

7. Taking charge 107

Acknowledgments 111

FOREWORD

Here's a recommended recipe for a book that would be well worth reading.

Take one ordinary Christian.

Add an experienced journalist with good writing and communication skills.

Mix with a thinking Bible student who has grappled with Scripture.

Introduce all three to a local pastor with plenty of experience in leading a church full of diverse people.

Put them all in a room with someone who lives and works in a tough, inner-city, multi-racial, multicultural community.

Stir and leave to settle for a number of years.

Finally, ask them to write a book together (combining their joint experience, skills, insights and expertise) on how to be yourself at the same time as living as a Christian in today's world.

Now you've really got a book worth reading!

That's exactly what *Dare to Break the Mould* is. Simon Jones is a committed Christian, a journalist, a theologian, a pastor, the leader of an inner-city church, and, take it from me, someone who understands the secular culture in which we are all called to live out our Christian faith today.

What you will find in the pages of this book are no neat, ivory-tower theories about Christian living developed by a remote scholar cushioned from real life. *Dare to Break the Mould* is honest and down to earth. It's full of practical and thoroughly biblical principles, with not a cliché in sight. It's written out of experience by someone who lives with his feet on the ground and who yet is a mould-breaker. And it's written in a style that's easy to read and relate to.

It sounds good, doesn't it? Well, it is, so get reading.

Steve Chalke
The Oasis Trust

INTRODUCTION

*b*reaking the mould

I remember standing, a young journalist, in the packed Connaught Rooms in London. The TV lights were ablaze, people with microphones jostled for position, and papers rustled as the assembled hacks leafed through press releases. Then, at one end of the hall, four figures took their places and announced that they were breaking the mould of British politics.

Roy Jenkins, David Owen, Shirley Williams and Bill Rogers, the so-called 'Gang of Four', were launching a major new political party which aimed to change the way politics was done in Britain.

The Social Democratic Party is now just a footnote to British political history. Some would say it wasn't needed. Others would say that it was unable to break out of the straitjacket of political life.

In his letter to the Christians at Rome, Paul urges *us* to break the mould. In J. B. Phillips' memorable translation of Romans 12:2, Paul says: 'Don't let the world around you squeeze you into its own mould, but let God remould your minds from within.'

We'll find it as hard, as the SDP did. But we have God working powerfully with us to enable us to succeed.

Normally we can rely on the support of our churches and Christian friends too. But

"Sometimes churches and friends try to squeeze us into their mould . . ."

sometimes those churches and friends, Christian media, books and convention speakers try to squeeze us into their mould rather than cooperate with God in his remoulding exercise.

Too often these days we're told what is and what isn't acceptable behaviour for a Christian. Too often we're told that if we want to get the blessing, to be in the vanguard of what God is up to in the world, then we need to do certain things, hold certain beliefs, worship in a certain way, and walk with God according to the ideas of the latest superstar author or convention speaker.

"But Jesus sets us free."

But Jesus sets us free. He does not expect us to swap the chains of sin, death and bondage to the spirit of the age for the chains of conformity to other people's image of an acceptable Christian in the 1990s. The requirement we have to conform to is the one we find in the Bible: that we walk with God in trust and obedience.

The advertisers urge, 'Be yourself'; the Government stresses 'freedom to choose'; rock singers scream that we should 'do our own thing'.

The trouble is, when the world says that, it generally means that we should be like everyone else, wearing the latest fashions, listening to the latest tunes, following the latest food fads, thinking the trendy thoughts. Only then will we be really free and happy. But so many people find that to be a heartbreaking lie.

"When God says 'Be yourself', he means it."

When God says 'Be yourself', however, he means it. As John Stott says: 'I am a unique person . . . My uniqueness is due to my genetic endowment, my inherited personality and temperament, my parentage, upbringing and education, my talents, inclinations and interests, my new birth and spiritual gifts. By the grace of God I am what I am.'

John Stott, *The Contemporary Christian*, (IVP), p. 144.

In the following pages we chart a course through the basic landscape of the Christian life: the quiet time, worship, handling questions and uncertainties, guidance, and the struggle with sin (our old nature). We start with the Bible, the key tool for breaking moulds, asking what it is and how we should read it. The other chapters apply mould-breaking biblical thinking to various areas of our lives.

So I dare you: get hold of the Bible and break out of the mould that the world – and occasionally the Christian world – tries to squeeze you into.

A word of thanks to Yvette, Mohan and Graham for reading parts of the book during the writing; to Oak Hall Holidays for the trip to Austria where the basic structure took shape as I talked with people from all sorts of church backgrounds; and to my church for the time and space to write. Where I refer to people by their Christian names by way of examples, those names are fictitious – except one: thanks to Nick for his support.

Finally, Linda, my wife, has been an invaluable source of ideas and gentle criticism. This book is dedicated to her and to our girls, Charlotte and Olivia, with thanks for their love and support for this Christian as he finds his way with God in the world.

OPENING THE BOOK

1

| C | H | A | P | T | E | R |

Sheila looked blankly at the page, pushing the hair off her cheeks. Suddenly a smile flickered on her lips. She looked up, eyes aglow with the satisfaction of having just solved a riddle. 'I see,' she said.

We had spents weeks looking at the Bible together. I had frequently left those sessions wondering how anyone so apparently bright and capable could be so obtuse. 'Isn't it obvious?' I exclaimed in exasperation to Linda as she revived me with a cup of coffee. 'How can anyone read Romans 5 and not see that we are accepted by God on the basis of our faith in what Jesus did on the cross, and that we don't have to do anything else?'

'Thousands do fail to see it,' Linda replied.

Romans 5:1–11

Now Sheila was beginning to understand.

The Bible is about as open a book to some people as astrophysics is to me. They look at it and it's dull, obscure, disordered, full of strange ideas and people with unpronounceable names. For those who have a high regard for this book – who view it as God's revelation of himself – this is immensely worrying and frustrating.

'I wish I understood more,' said Duncan, choking back the tears, 'but I open it and so much is weird. Why does Paul spend so much time talking about meat in 1 Corinthians? How relevant is that to me? I'm not a butcher or a vegetarian! How do I make sense of Ezekiel, Isaiah and Revelation?'

"How is that relevant to me?"

Like this mature Christian man, all of us have read a passage of Scripture and thought, 'What's this all about, then?' But for many of us, brought up to believe that we only need the Holy Spirit to make Scripture plain to us, this is a problem. If we're Christians, we have the Holy Spirit; if Scripture isn't plain, then, we think something must be wrong with us.

The key is to understand what *kind* of book it is we're reading.

"The key is to understand what kind of book it is we're reading."

a book full of stories

The speaker closed his large black Bible, clasped it close to his heart, lowered his voice and said: 'If you want to operate a microwave, you follow the instructions in the maker's manual. If you want to live properly, you must follow the instructions in the Maker's manual, the Bible. If your life's not working, look it up in the manual and you'll find an answer there . . .'

I have a number of makers' manuals in my house covering all sorts of domestic appliances. The thickest and most detailed is the *Haynes' Workshop Manual* my father-in-law gave me when I acquired a Vauxhall Cavalier. The manual is a mine of information on stripping down engines, fault-finding and correcting, and replacing bits that drop off or wear out. I've looked at it a couple of times, but I need a guide to understanding the manual! I am to car maintenance what Eddie 'the Eagle' Edwards is to ski-jumping.

I do not consider the Bible, however, to be a manual. Life is not like a car. If something goes wrong, you can't just open it up to see what's happened and adjust it with a spanner. The kind of problems we face are not in the same league as faulty carburettors or cracked manifolds.

The Bible is a book. But it is not a manual or an A to Z of life with God. It is not a 'how to' book. You know the sort of thing I mean: *How to Lose Weight in Three Months While Still Eating Cream Cakes*, or *How to Get Extremely Rich While Working Only Six Hours a Day*. It is not a recipe book: 'Take one life, add regular church attendance, membership of a home group and a daily quiet time; allow to simmer for seventy years, then take upstairs.'

The Bible is a *story* book. It is the story of God's involvement with the world he made. It is the story of God's relationship with the people he created, a relationship marked by ups and downs, spanning generations, involving war, conquest, betrayal, love, sex,

" . . . the story of God's involvement with the world he made . . ."

God has given us a book
   full of stories,
   Which was made for
   his people of old,
It begins with the tale of a
   garden
   And ends with the
   city of gold.
      Maria Penstone

business, defeats, victories and death, a relationship that leads people from the depths of sin and alienation to the glorious heights of a renewed planet and eternal life. It is a ripping yarn!

The whole Bible is a story, and, like all good stories, it has a plot, characters, a beginning and an ending. Like all good stories, it engages the emotions as well as the intellect. What is the Bible about? What is the plot that runs from Genesis to Revelation? It can be summed up in a sentence: The Bible is about God's love for the world he made and the people he put in it, and how he rescued them.

Within that main story, of course, there are lots of little stories. For the Bible is not a single book, but a *library* of books, a collection put together over hundreds of years. All these books contribute to the overall story of God's love affair with the world he made.

*g*etting into the story

'The Bible is much more than a book,' the preacher thundered. 'It is nothing less than the Word of God.'

Absolutely. But the Bible *is* a book. We evangelicals have been so keen to stress that it's more than a book, and that it is God-breathed and therefore not like any other book we'll ever read, that we have in effect treated it as *less* than a book. We don't *read* it; we *use* it. We don't get into it and allow its story to fill our thinking and imagination. Instead, we turn to it when we need advice, help, a word for this situation, a text for that.

"We don't get into it and allow its story to fill our thinking . . ."

Nearly everyone loves a good story. We read novels, from pulp fiction to the classics. We go to the movies, get engrossed in TV soaps, and listen to friends' tales of holidays or misfortunes with the car. We share our life story with the people we love, and recite timeless tales to our children as we tuck them into bed. Stories can make us fall about laughing or curl up crying. They can capture the reality of a situation in a way that mere reporting or a philosophical treatise cannot.

This fact was brought home to me afresh when I read two books by C. S. Lewis, the great Christian thinker of the thirties, forties and fifties. He published a book in 1940 called *The Problem of Pain*, in which he brought his searing intellect to bear on humanity's most pressing and perennial problem. It is a marvellous book, full of clear argument and practical wisdom.

But it is a little cold, a mite clinical. In 1961 he published, anonymously at first, *A Grief Observed* – the powerful story of how he coped with the loss of his beloved wife. At sixty pages it is less than half the length of his earlier work. Yet it packs the kind of punch *The Problem of Pain* never came close to. Why? Because it is a *story*. As we read it we are absorbed by it, we become involved in its action, caught up in its emotion, and thus lifted to a new understanding of ourselves and of the God we love, as Lewis himself was.

God knows how important stories are to each one of us. So he chose to address us in a story – the story of a nation, chosen to be the agent through which he would work out his plan to rescue the planet and its inhabitants.

And within that big story are lots of little stories about ordinary people living ordinary lives, and extraordinary people living extraordinary lives.

Stories like the life of Jacob; the career of Joseph; the ups, downs and ups of Moses. The lovely story of Ruth, the loyal daughter-in-law, the stranger in a foreign land who finds love and fulfilment as she struggles to do what is right by her family and her God. The fascinating story of Esther; the inspiring story of Nehemiah and Ezra; the heartbreaking soap opera of David; the traumatic struggle of Job. The list goes on and on.

Within the story there is great poetry, including the Psalms, which voice the response of the faithful to all God's dealings with them, pleasurable and otherwise. There are the offbeat musings of the preacher in Ecclesiastes, the story of how a wry, slightly cynical man comes to grips with faith in the real world. And there is the powerful, explicit love song of Solomon. All human life is here.

Then there's the story of a carpenter who becomes a preacher, attracts a crowd, stirs up a controversy, and begins a movement that will change the face of the world. It's a story that plumbs the darkest depths of betrayal, failure, suffering and death before it soars to the ecstatic heights of victory, joy and life, the triumph of good over evil.

And there's the story of the young church, stumbling and sprinting like an energetic toddler across the pages of history; a story of solid achievements and heart-rending setbacks, of inspiring saints and all-too-earthbound sinners. Finally, there's the story of the most amazing wedding ever seen, fol-

"The Holy Spirit knew what he was doing when he inspired so much of the Bible in the form of narrative."
Fee and Stuart

lowed by the universe's longest-running party.

The Bible is an extraordinary book!

Who's who and what's what?

Paul tells Timothy: 'Do your best to present yourself to God as . . . a worker who has no need to be ashamed, rightly explaining the word of truth.' We need to take this advice on board. As with any story, especially one from another time and culture, the Bible needs to be worked at if we are going to get the best from it.

2 Timothy 2:15

Because it is a story, we need, first, to work at understanding the characters. We need to pay attention to how the plot develops – how the story moves on from, for instance, Abraham to Isaac to Jacob, to Israel being enslaved in Egypt, and to God's dramatic intervention.

As the story moves on, we need to note what God is doing, and what he is showing us about himself and about how he wants us to relate to him. This is not always straightforward. Take the story of David from the time he consolidates power to the moment of his death, when he hands the kingdom over to Solomon. This is a breathtaking piece of storytelling. The characters are sharply observed; the events are recounted with an eye for detail and a subtlety of pace that many modern storytellers would do well to mimic.

2 Samuel 9 – 20 and 1 Kings 1 – 2; 'The court history of David' or 'the succession narrative'.

But through the whole story we constantly find ourselves asking, 'Where is God? Whose side is he on?' Apart from when Nathan comes to David after the sin with Bathsheba,

God remains in the background and leaves us to work out precisely where he is in the story, and how he is working. And that is the genius of this type of writing; for as we become involved in the story of David, caught up in the manoeuvring and machinations of his family, asking, with the characters, 'What will happen next?' and 'What does God want?' so we begin to draw parallels between David's story and ours. We come to see more clearly what God is doing in our own lives, and how he is involved in the world in which we daily spend our lives.

"Consecutive reading of biblical books forces everyone who wants to hear to put himself, or allow himself to be found, where God has acted once and for all for the salvation of men."
Dietrich Bonhoeffer

*g*ot the guidebook, dear?

Secondly, because the Bible comes from a time and culture different from ours, we need to work at understanding the background in which the stories are set.

I'm a sucker for old buildings. Not only do I live in one and work in another, but regularly, from the spring to the autumn, I pack my family and National Trust card into the car and go off to view some crumbling monument. We love it – squeezing through low doors, winding up spiral staircases, peering into vast open fireplaces, sniffing the atmosphere and trying to imagine what life was like in the building's heyday.

"... and go off to view some crumbling monument ..."

As I walk round a country house, I'm brimming with questions: Why is that there? What was that used for? Who lived here? When were the various bits built? Why were the newer parts added on to an existing structure? How? Why are the doors so low; were people really shorter in those days?

20

I can answer many of these questions out of my sparse knowledge of history and limited common sense. But sometimes I'm stumped.

Wandering in the billiard room at Ightham Mote in Kent, we came upon a small doorway that opened on to a flight of steps leading straight down into the moat. What was it for? Maybe before the room was used for billiards it was a store room, and supplies were brought in by boat across the water. Maybe it was an escape route in case the house was overrun by enemies. Was it a bizzare version of a priest-hole? I was baffled.

The guidebook came to the rescue.

The great thing about almost all National Trust and English Heritage properties is that an expert in the history and architecture of each particular building has produced a guidebook to it. And almost without fail the guidebook answers every question that my common sense and smattering of history cannot.

The door in the billiard room at Ightham Mote and the stairs that go down into the moat are there 'for bathing purposes', says the guidebook. Simple, when you know.

"The Bible is, in many ways, like a country house."

The Bible is, in many ways, like a country house. It is old. It has been added to through the years. It is open for us to walk round and view. Many of the questions we have about the Bible we can answer ourselves through our common sense – which is God-given and not entirely wrecked by the fall – and through the knowledge we've picked up along the way by going to church and talking to other Christians.

DARE TO BREAK THE MOULD

Leviticus 19:19
Deuteronomy 22:8;
14:21
Ruth 3 – 4
Proverbs 23:1–11
1 Corinthians 8 – 10
Revelation 13

But parts of the Bible are obscure. As we read it, we come across laws that forbid the wearing of mixed fibres, demand that we all have parapets on our roofs, and outlaw the boiling of a kid in its mother's milk. We stumble over odd marriage customs. We fall into strange sayings about eating with the rich and not moving boundary markers. We read passionate passages about meat and worship, and encounter strange beasts that emerge from the sea and from the earth, spilling numbers in profusion all around them.

We need help. And just as there are guidebooks to country houses and castles, so there are guidebooks to the Bible. We need to make use of them. The Holy Spirit has raised up men and women skilled in history, archaeology and ancient languages, and gifted to teach – both verbally and through books. God intends us to make use of them.

We are very fortunate in our society to have a wealth of Bible study aids available. It seems to me that all serious readers of the Bible – that is, all Christians who want to grow in their understanding of God, themselves and the life of faith they have embarked on – need to have a Bible handbook, an atlas, a Bible dictionary and commentary, and a concordance (a sort of index to the whole Bible). Details of helpful ones can be found in the list at the end of the chapter.

*S*pot that plot!

Thirdly, we need to work at reading the Bible carefully within a framework.

I love the cinema. Well, these days, prices being what they are, I should say I love the video. When I see a film I have a pretty good idea what I should expect. I'll have read a review, heard Barry Norman's verdict on the telly, talked to a mate who's seen it. If it's a western, then, from previous westerns I've seen, I know there'll be good guys and bad guys, and possibly native Americans. There will be something about the pioneering spirit and the conflict between that and the need for law and order. If I didn't have any of that background I probably wouldn't know what to make of a western at all. The same is true of romantic comedies: I don't expect people to be shot in the opening sequence, or hideous monsters to rise out of a grave seeking revenge, because neither belongs in romantic comedy.

"I don't expect people to be shot in the opening sequence . . ."

Likewise, when I come to the Bible, I have a framework. I know something already about God, Jesus and the church, and the context in which the particular book or chapter I'm reading belongs. I have a growing understanding of the plan of salvation, of the way the story unfolds from Genesis to Jesus to Revelation. I will come to everything I read with that background. This is important, as the following examples will, I hope, show.

'I don't get why Paul is so down on marriage and women.' Jackie was speaking calmly, but there was an edge of anger in her tone. Clearly she felt hurt in some way by what she understood Paul to be saying in 1 Corinthians 7 – all the more so as she was looking forward very much to marrying the man she loved.

'But 1 Corinthians 7 isn't really about marriage,' I said as gently as I could. 'It's about sex and why married people shouldn't give it up. And it's about thinking for yourself whether you should get married in view of the circumstances you are living in. Paul leaves the decision up to each individual.'

'I've never heard that before,' she said, a note of hope creeping into her voice. 'How do you know that's what Paul meant?'

I explained about the background to 1 Corinthians. The church in Corinth was having problems with teaching that so emphasized the spiritual that it neglected people's physical needs, to the extent that married people were told to stop having sex. I added that, for Paul, the whole notion of Christian freedom was very important, and that part of the fruit that the Holy Spirit grows in each Christian is self-control, the ability to make decisions for ourselves as we grow up in Christ.

There's a lot more to it than that, of course. But the point is that some background knowledge – available in Bible handbooks and commentaries – is vital for properly understanding what the text is saying.

"... the ability to make decisions for ourselves as we grow up in Christ."

Mark 13:7 – note carefully what Jesus actually says!

'You can't work for peace in this world because Jesus said there would be wars and rumours of wars right up to the time of his return.'

Gordon broke off, though he had clearly intended to say more. I had started gagging visibly at this point, in complete disbelief! Gordon was deadly serious. I suggested that Jesus wasn't *commanding* us to make war until his return, but merely pointing out that this was the way of the world.

Far from war being his will until his return, he was keen to see his followers engage in peacemaking – after all, one of the great benefits of the salvation the Bible talks of is peace.

We need to view individual passages or sayings in the light of what the whole story is about. Each text must be seen in context or it becomes a pretext.

"To appreciate Scripture, as with other great literature, we must begin by receiving the text in the way it was intended."
Michael Christenson

We need a framework for understanding each section of the story, otherwise we will be in danger of leaping to odd and dangerous conclusions. We call this framework a *theology* – a way of thinking about God, his world and his work in it. And developing a theology is a vital part of our growth as Christians.

*a*ll together, now!

Fourthly, we need to work at the Bible with other people. The Christian life is not like the life of a lone yachtswoman circumnavigating the globe. We need to read the Bible in fellowship with others; that's why we go to church and to home groups. We need to chat with other Christians over things that we don't understand or which cause us difficulty, because their experience, insight and wisdom are invaluable to us (as ours are to them).

When I prepare a sermon I sit at my desk with my commentaries open around my Bible. Though I am on my own, I am not alone. In a very real sense I am in fellowship with the world of scholarship and Christian experience that produced all those commentaries. I am not conjuring sermons out of my imagination, however inspired. I am working in partnership with other, more knowledgeable Christians, and with the Holy Spirit, to interpret the Word of God correctly and proclaim it intelligibly.

*S*uck it and see!

Fifthly, we need to read the Bible in a variety of ways. Sometimes it is good to read long sections at one sitting – whole books, or whole stories such as the life of Joseph or the story of the exodus. At other times it is good to read a chapter or a paragraph more closely, paying attention to the fine detail. Sometimes it is helpful to concentrate on just one word.

See Psalm 1:2

The Psalms speak frequently of meditating on the law or word of God. This is something we need to rediscover in our instant-coffee culture. Meditation is about making a meal of what we read. In Isaiah 31:4 the prophet uses the word 'meditate' to describe what lions do with a kill. They purr over it, delight in it, take their time with it, and ensure they get every bit of nourishment out of each morsel. We should do the same with Scripture.

". . . making a meal of what we read . . ."

Meditating on it is a bit like sucking a sweet. As we move it around our mouth and explore its surface with our tongue, it changes shape and texture. To get the most out of the Bible we need to do that with what we read. We need to think about how a particular word applies to each and every area of our life, ponder the shades of meaning that it has, and tease out what difference reading this passage is going to make to us today.

*K*eeping the goal in focus

People frequently complain that they are not getting anything out of the Bible. I tend to ask them two questions: 'What are you looking for?' and 'How are you looking?'

Christians have traditionally described the Bible as God's revelation of himself. The Bible is a book about God. So when I read it I should expect to find out about him, his character, his way of working, his dealings with the world, and his way of looking at things. I should be looking for God. If I go to the Bible asking only, 'What's in this for me?' I'm going to miss a great deal, and so stunt my growth as a Christian (as we'll see in the next chapter).

As to how we should read it, it's as well to remember what's written on the front of every Bible I've ever owned: *Holy*.

We must come to read this remarkable, wonderful, awe-inspiring book in an attitude of reverence. We don't come casually, thinking, 'Oh, I know this bit; I'll skip that!' We need to come humbly, carefully, thoughtfully. We need to mull over what it's saying, ponder it, treat the words with respect and realize that at the end of the day I do not sit in judgment on the Bible; it sits in judgment on me.

So I need to be very cautious about actions based on a verse here or a passage there – as we shall see in chapter 4. God doesn't play dice with us, and we shouldn't with Scripture.

God has given us a book full of stories to enjoy and respond to. Reading it is a vital part of the adventure of faith to which God has called us. So let's go to it with relish and gusto.

Some helpful books

The basic kit for helping us read the Bible to the full consists of the following: a study Bible (the NIV study Bible by Hodder and Stoughton is excellent); a concordance; a Bible handbook (the *Lion Handbook* is available in paperback, so it is not only very helpful but good value too); a Bible dictionary, such as IVP's *New Concise Bible Dictionary*; a one-volume commentary, such as IVP's *New Bible Commentary*; and an atlas such as the *New Bible Atlas*, again by IVP.

John Drane's *Introduction to the Bible* (Lion) is extremely helpful, as is Steve Motyer's *Unlock the Bible*, and *How to Read the Bible for All its Worth* by Gordon Fee and Douglas Stuart (both these from Scripture Union).

The Old Testament is often seen as presenting particular problems because of its many difficulties and obscure passages. There are a number of helpful introductions to studying it. Among them are David Burke, *From Genesis to Jesus* and E. P. Clowney, *The Unfolding Mystery* (both from IVP).

Philip Yancey's *Seeing in the Dark* (Marshall Pickering) is a wonderful trip through the story of the Bible by one of today's best Christian writers.

There are a number of good commentary series on individual books of the Bible, for more detailed and advanced study – especially helpful for those of us asked to lead Bible studies at church, school, work or college. IVP publishes a good series called the *Tyndale Commentaries*, which is complete for the New Testament and getting there for the Old. For the background to 1 Corinthians 7 referred to in the chapter, see Gordon Fee's commentary in the *New International Commentary on the New Testament* series, and David Prior's exposition in *The Bible Speaks Today* series from IVP.

GETTING TO KNOW YOU

C H A P T E R

It was the first night of the Christian Union houseparty. I was in bed, propped up on one elbow, Bible open, notebook at the ready, notes to hand. My room-mate, Gerald, came in singing, looked at me, and remarked scornfully, 'Don't tell me you put your armour on *before you go to sleep!* There's no point getting ready for battle and then going off duty!'

His tone of voice strongly suggested I was endangering my salvation. I could only stammer some vague response about not having had time until now, and not wanting to get too far behind. I didn't have the heart to tell him I was so far behind that I was still using

". . . write me off as a hopeless case . . ."

the last quarter's notes, for fear that he'd knowingly raise his eyebrows, tut and write me off as a hopeless case.

The 'quiet time' seems to cause more disquiet among faithful Christians than just about anything else. We are told we must have a daily time with the Lord, reading Scripture and praying, if we want to grow and develop in our Christian lives.

'Read your Bible, pray every day if you want to grow,' goes the chorus I used to lead my Crusader class in singing. Trouble is, more often than not I wasn't, and hadn't been for a while, and felt wretchedly guilty as every word crept past my lips.

There have been times in my Christian life when I have rebelled against the QT (yes, confession is good for all of us!). I haven't bought any of those attractively packaged notes (not that these aren't excellent publications); I haven't risen with the lark to start the day with Jesus. The truth is, I'm not able to focus that early in the morning, let alone do anything remotely difficult like read and talk! And I haven't felt guilty about it – well, not very guilty.

See Psalm 1

To be honest, I have always been uncertain about what the QT is for, and what its value is. These uncertainties have been reinforced over the years by conversations with friends who find the daily discipline difficult to keep up, the resources available bland and unrewarding, and the whole process one that produces guilt rather than developing a deeper relationship with God. Some have told me how hard they find it to learn from books; some that they miss the stimulation of other people.

I in my small corner

The QT is a product of the evangelical church's historical and necessary emphasis on the individual and her or his relationship with God. That accounts for both its strengths and weaknesses.

Reading Scripture and praying regularly undoubtedly build spiritual muscle. Recently I went to see my doctor for an MOT on my body. In the course of our conversation, as he pulled and tweaked parts of my anatomy, he asked, 'How often do you get out of breath?'

'Every time I go upstairs,' I replied.

'No, I mean, how often are you out of breath for half for an hour or more?'

I thought for a moment and then responded firmly, 'Every time I go upstairs!'

He did well to hide his exasperation. He patiently explained that I ought to do some kind of exercise that ensured I was out of breath for half an hour three times a week, as this exercised the heart and developed stamina.

'Cardiovascular exercise is vital,' he warned, getting technical probably to intimidate me into obeying him, 'especially to someone who leads a sedentary life as you do.'

'Thanks a lot, doctor,' I thought, 'you think I'm a lazy slob who's going to die of a heart attack before I'm fifty.' But I got his point, took his advice, and bought an exercise bike. Now I get out of breath every time I look at it.

" . . . cardiovascular exercise for the soul . . ."

The quiet time is cardiovascular exercise for the soul, vital for developing spiritual muscles. Looking back over what I have learned in my Christian life, I've learned much of it on my own by reading the Bible, thinking about it and praying.

Matthew 6:5–6

I remember the feeling of near-elation when, as a young Christian, I realized that I could pray on my own, and that I didn't need to be in church or with the youth group to talk to God. I was at a houseparty. It was the middle of the night and I was lying awake in bed worrying (I can't remember what about – probably school or a girl, because that was all I ever worried about at that time). Suddenly I thought – or maybe God said to me – 'Why don't you pray about it?' So I did. And I've not looked back since. I pray in all sorts of places about anything and everything.

The quiet time can also be a major source of our knowledge of the Bible. The more you read the more you remember. It's a bit like osmosis, really. If you dip the corner of a sheet of blotting-paper in water and leave it there, eventually the whole sheet will be wet because the water will have been drawn up by the porous material. That's osmosis.

I had an economics teacher at school who told me that the only way I'd learn any economics was by opening the textbook. 'It's no good stuffing it under your arm, Jones, and trusting osmosis,' he said. And of course he was right. But *reading* is a bit like osmosis: the more you read passages, the more they are drawn up into your memory and stick there. For this reason it is often good, as part of a quiet time, to attempt to memorize Scripture. There are many aids to help in this.

Jesus clearly knew Scripture. And he can only have known it through personal, detailed and devoted study of it. When Satan tempted him by quoting Scripture at him –

always out of context – Jesus always replied by quoting Scripture *in* context.

*W*e can work it out

Jesus, of course, probably never had a Bible of his own.

Huh? What rampant heresy is this? If Jesus never had a Bible, how could he have had a quiet time? Well, he probably never had a quiet time in the way we're encouraged to. And much of his knowledge and understanding of Scripture would have come from studying with others. Personal study is not necessarily private study.

Private study, unlike praying on your own, can be very isolating. It can leave me feeling that when I come across any difficulty in my reading, I have to solve it or find a way round it by myself. It can also be very dangerous; I can jump to all sorts of ludicrous conclusions about a passage of Scripture if I study it *solely* on my own, justifying my conclusions by claiming that the Holy Spirit spoke to me as I was at my personal devotions.

The emphasis on learning via the quiet time can be very threatening to non-readers, and to those who can read but don't. For these people the QT can be a major source of guilt.

'Do you read your Bible *every* day?' Maxine asked in a timid voice.

I tried to be non-committal because I knew what was coming next. 'I can't concentrate for long enough,' she went on, 'and I don't understand a lot of it. Praying is easy, cos that's just talking to God, but reading the

Luke 4:4, 8, 12, all quoted from Deuteronomy – the focus of Jesus' meditations in the wilderness?

"Jesus probably never had a Bible . . ."

".. . to see how to cook spaghetti bolognese . . ."

Colossians 3:16

Bible is something else . . .'

This woman isn't thick. She's perceptive, and aware of what's going on in the world and in her neighbourhood. She keeps up with current events by watching television. If she wants to find out about something, she asks someone who knows. She doesn't go to the library and get a book on it, as I would. She can read, but doesn't. She certainly doesn't read to learn, except maybe a recipe book to see how to cook spaghetti bolognese.

She, and many others like her, find the whole notion of a quiet time threatening. Yet she bubbles with guilt because she has got the impression that you can't be a good, sound, first-class Christian unless you have a daily QT. People like Maxine can grow as Christians by listening to the Bible on tape, and by being involved in a home group where people learn together. We'll return to this issue later.

For those of us who do enjoy reading, great care must be taken over *how* we read the Bible. Because the focus of the QT tends to be on *me*, *my* spiritual development, and the growth of *my* understanding, it tends to make us read the Bible with only one question in mind: what is this passage saying to *me*?

Don't get me wrong. I want God to speak to me through Scripture. I want to hear his voice. But this can become such an obsession that we miss what the Bible is saying about other things, like God, the world, the Christian faith in general, the society we live in, the companies we work for, the schools we teach in, and so on. God is not going to speak directly to me about me every day. But the Bible has a lot to say about God, the world in which I live, and how I relate to them – probably enough for something new every week.

*h*e ain't heavy, he's my brother

The Christian life is about being the individuals God made us to be in the community in which he has put us. No-one is an island. There is no such thing as a solo Christian. We cannot learn solely on our own, and so we should always see our personal devotional life, vital though it is, as but one of the means by which we grow.

Of course, most of us already know this. We therefore go to church every week, celebrations once in a while, and maybe a convention like Spring Harvest every year. These are all places where we learn things, develop our spiritual muscles, and grow up as people of faith.

We need each other. All through the Bible there is great stress on people together. Listen to American pastor Eugene Peterson: 'In the presence of God, "alone" is not good . . . Call a friend. "Where two or three are gathered together in my name, there am I in the midst of them." By ourselves, we are not ourselves. Solitary confinement is extreme punishment.'

Matthew 18:20 (AV)

Of course, we pray on our own, Peterson continues, in all places at all times. But we must also pray together. We need an equal emphasis on *both*. The great prayers of the Bible, the Psalms, aren't personal, private prayers. They are shared prayers, he says.

E.g. Psalm 122

Eugene H. Peterson, *Answering God: the Psalms as Tools for Prayer* (Harper-Collins), p. 18.

". . . we jog one another along when our zeal is lacking . . ."

1 Corinthians 12 – a picture of glorious diversity!

'All the psalms are prayers in community: people assembled, attentive before God, participating in a common posture, movement and speech, offering themselves and each other to their Lord. Prayer is not a private exercise but a family convocation' (that is, a get-together with other members of the family of faith).

When we pray together we inspire each other, and jog one another along when our zeal or enthusiasm or energy is lacking. Often listening to another brother or sister praying a short prayer from the heart draws us nearer to God than a whole night alone on our knees could do. So there is much to be said for praying regularly in pairs and triplets and groups.

The same applies to reading Scripture. One reason we go to church is so that we can learn. Sermons and talks are meant to teach. (The fact that many don't is not the fault of the form, but of the preacher!) The reason for the growth and popularity of home groups over recent years is that they are a great way of learning from the Bible. In a small group, ideas can be tossed around, insights can be shared, and light can be thrown on a particular passage in a way that can't happen when you're reading the Bible on your own, even with study aids.

The great thing about churches is that they are made up of all kinds of people with all kinds of experiences of life, the world, faith and God. All these different kinds of people, filled with the Holy Spirit, have a part to play in teaching us about how we can live better Christian lives.

If we made full use of what goes on at

church on Sundays and during the week, perhaps it would take the pressure off the quiet time. Then, instead of it feeling like a straitjacket that we have to squeeze ourselves into, trying to smile despite the discomfort, it would become the means through which we got to know God better – which, after all, is the point of the exercise.

It is good to have a time for quiet reflection regularly through the week – though there is no magic about doing it every day. It does, however, need to be planned. It will never just happen. There is a helpful discipline in the QT – 'Read your Bible, pray *every day*' – for it stresses that we must make time to meet God. We can always find time to meet a girlfriend or boyfriend, however busy we are. Fans of *EastEnders* and *Coronation Street* religiously drop what they're doing and turn on at the appointed time. Isn't meeting God enjoyable and vital, and worth making a priority? Get your diary out and schedule a week's devotions now.

Sometimes the available minutes could be spent reading the Bible and praying. At other times you could go for a walk and talk to God about what you see. I live in the middle of run-down council estates, but even here there are trees and clouds, laughing children and chatting neighbours, colourful advertising and litter, all of which I can talk to God about while I'm walking.

". . . talk to God about what you see . . ."

At other times you could read another Christian book or magazine. Spending time reading *The Practice of the Presence of God* or *The Pilgrim's Progress* can be a valuable way of getting to know God better. Or you could try responding to God through some creative art: drawing, music, poetry.

Another alternative is to spend the time listening to Christians speaking about their faith. How much we have to learn from those who have been walking with God since before we were born! Sometimes this could be done face to face, sometimes via tapes and videos; there is an ever-expanding pool to dip into.

Perhaps none of these appeal to you. But they may be worth at least trying. Things that don't instantly appeal often turn out to be richly rewarding. On a trip to Austria I noticed that my itinerary included white-water rafting. This held no appeal for me at all. Being thrown about over icy-cold shallow rapids with nothing but a wetsuit to protect me from the rocks and hypothermia was not exactly my idea of a relaxing day out. But I went – I didn't want others on the trip saying the preacher was a chicken. And I loved it. It was exhausting and exhilarating, wet and wonderful. I want to do it again.

So try things you haven't tried before with your QT. It'll open new doors to God and prevent you becoming bored by doing the same thing day in, day out.

But remember: we should not stray too far from the Bible. The Bible should always be the focus of our growing understanding of God and our relationship with him. All these other suggestions should be seen and used as ways of bringing us back to the Bible with renewed enthusiasm. A week should not pass when we don't read a good chunk of Scripture.

I frequently talk to people who complain that they are stuck in a rut or feel as if they are on a treadmill. 'I do my notes every day,' Mandy said, 'but it's more out of a sense of duty than anything else.'

That is so sad. Jesus came to set us free. He wants to have a vibrant, lively, growing relationship with each one of us. And if the QT has become just a ritual – something that we do because it's there, or because we feel we must, or because our leaders tell us to, or because peer pressure makes us feel guilty if we don't – then it will stifle rather than liberate us.

" . . . more out of a sense of duty than anything else . . ."

Read Matthew 11:28–30

Simply changing the way we approach the Bible can often breathe new life into our quiet times. Following set readings can tend to chop Scripture up into bite-sized chunks and give us snacks rather than meals. Often I find it helpful to read a whole book or a whole chapter rather than just a few verses. Of course, we need to do both to ensure that we have a balanced diet.

If I am finding it hard to pray, then reading a sizeable portion of Scripture will frequently give me plenty to talk to God about, and the words will begin to flow more easily – often words of praise followed by confession and laughter. Why, I wonder, didn't I just talk to God when he was there at my shoulder all the time, eager to start a conversation?

When we can't put our feelings into words to God, then the Psalms are there to help us. Psalms often express what we cannot or dare not. Regularly reading and praying them gives us a whole new vocabulary to use in getting to know God better.

I'll do it my way

Read Psalm 19:7–14

God wants us to get to know him better. This amazing truth is what makes having a creative and satisfying quiet time such a fulfilling experience.

There are few things as enjoyable as having a good meal with friends – the laughter, the variety of tastes, the feeling of being physically full with excellent food and wine, emotionally and intellectually full with the chat, the exchange of ideas and jokes, and spiritually full with the feeling and reality of having grown in our relationship with these people. Surely that's why Jesus spent so much time at dinner parties.

That's really how a quiet time should feel. It is our chance to eat and drink, to talk and laugh, to be noisy and silent with God. At meals with friends we can be ourselves, relaxed and uninhibited. Likewise in our quiet time we can be ourselves in God's presence: sometimes noisy with happiness, sometimes reflective and quiet with questions and uncertainties; sometimes noisy with anger and perplexity; sometimes quietly thrilled at his goodness and our sense of well-being.

". . . we have to slip the bonds of guilt over the QT."

For this to happen, we have to slip the bonds of guilt over the QT. We have to remind ourselves that the quiet time was made for us, not us for the quiet time. So it's all right to work out the best way, for us, of getting to know God better.

'*I* once read something helpful about that'

On prayer and the devotional life I have found the following helpful: Richard Foster, *Celebration of Discipline* (Hodder and Stoughton); Paul Wallis, *Rough Ways in Prayer* (Triangle); James Houston, *The Transforming Friendship* (Lion); John White, *People in Prayer* (IVP); and Bill Hybels, *Too Busy Not to Pray* (IVP).

Among Bible study aids that I use from time to time are *Alive to God*, *Daily Notes* and *Daily Bread* (all by Scripture Union). CWR publish *Every Day with Jesus*. John Pitchford's *Daily with God* (Canterbury Press) is very liturgical but I've found much blessing in its discipline.

Stephen Eyre's *Spiritual Encounters* (Frameworks), a month's-worth of guided meditations, is very helpful. Ro Willoughby's *Adventure with God* (IVP) enables people to cover the Bible in two years, using a variety of approaches to daily study. Eddie Askew has produced six excellent books of Bible readings with accompanying meditations. Available from the Leprosy Mission, they are called *A Silence and a Shouting*; *Disguises of Love*; *Many Voices, One Voice*; *No Strange Land*; *Facing the Storm* and *Breaking the Rules*.

John Bunyan's *The Pilgrim's Progress* (many editions) is still well worth reading, as are Dietrich Bonhoeffer's *Life Together* (SCM) and Thomas Kelly's *A Testament of Devotion* (Quaker Home Service). Hodder and Stoughton publish many excellent devotional books in their *Christian Classics* series. Dip into it.

Grove Books publish some useful pamphlets in its Grove Spirituality series: details from Grove Books, Bramcote, Nottingham NG9 3DS, UK.

I think the two most helpful books I have read on using the Bible to deepen my understanding of and relationship with God are Eugene Peterson's *Answering God: The Psalms as Tools for Prayer* and Philip Yancey's *Seeing in the Dark* (both HarperCollins). If you read nothing else apart from the Bible, read these!

ONCE MORE, WITH FEELING

3

'I don't believe these people. How long will they keep quenching the Spirit?' Michael paced up and down. 'They quibble over not being able to see the OHP, not knowing which song we're singing or what's happening next. Only the Spirit knows what's happening next! Don't they know that?' He threw up his hands in exasperation.

'Well, you know, there's more than one way . . .' I began.

But he was off again. 'There's no life in all that old stuff in the hymnbook,' he declared. 'Isn't it great when we've sung a song a few times and then we just carry on singing in the

Spirit, all contributing something different, tongues, the works . . .?'

I put away my queries and withdrew discreetly from the conversation.

'What I can't stand is the arrogance of these people!' Oh dear, I thought, Peggy's off. 'You can't read the words on the screen. I don't see what's wrong with hymnbooks. You never know what's coming next. Each song is ended by a lot of strumming and babble. I never know what to do. And the songs! Why can't we sing a hymn with good meaty content instead of these tuneless ditties that tell everyone how happy we are . . .?'

I'd been in this conversation before and not got anywhere, so I put my tambourine away and changed the subject.

". . . ditties that tell everyone how happy we are . . ."

Nothing seems to divide Christians like worship. It's not just that we can't agree on what we should sing. It seems that we're not always sure that we're even arguing over the same thing.

And what does God think? Well, sometimes I reckon he tiptoes out of a hymn-prayer sandwich service for fear of waking everyone up by his presence, and that he retreats from the chorusburger'n' tongues-shake knees-up because he can't get a word in edgeways.

Of course, it shouldn't be like this.

*O*h, it's heaven on earth

Worship doesn't really consist of just singing or praying, raising our hands or reading Scripture. Worship has more to do with sunbathing.

ONCE MORE, WITH FEELING

When the sun bursts through the slate-grey English sky, everyone dusts off their shorts, finds the sticky remains of last year's suntan lotion, and heads for the beach or the park. The really serious sun-seeker has a mat, little plastic eye-protectors and a grim determination to get every single ray on offer.

If we want a tan, we've got to put ourselves in a position to get the most sun: strip off, oil up and lie down. And first and foremost that is what worship is. The songs and liturgy, prayers and readings, hand-raising and sermon-listening are secondary to the initial and vital act of putting ourselves in the right place before God.

Worship is a shift of allegiance, of loyalty and service, away from ourselves and our possessions and our needs, to God. 'You shall have no other gods besides me,' boomed the Lord on Mount Sinai as he gave the Ten Commandments. Then, having scared the life out of the Israelites with the smoke and thunder, the lightning and the trumpet, he re-emphasized the seriousness of worship as an act of allegiance by warning them against idolatry of any kind; that is, the worship of anything or anyone other than the Lord their God.

Exodus 20:3 margin, 18–26

This means, of course, that worship is not what is on my lips but what's in my heart. And immediately we begin to see that worship is not just what happens in church on Sunday and at the midweek meeting or home group. It is also what happens at the kitchen sink, in the office, behind the wheel of my car, in conversation with my friends, and when I am planning how to spend my money. Worship is a matter of lifestyle.

"We should give ourselves to God in temporal and spiritual matters alike."
Brother Lawrence

Amos 5:21–23
Isaiah 1:12–17
Mark 7:6–7

This point is forcefully driven home by Amos, Isaiah, Jesus and Paul. 'I hate, I despise your festivals,' thundered God through Amos. '. . . Take away from me the noise of your songs; I will not listen to the melody of your harps.' Jesus quoted Isaiah to the religious leaders of his day: 'This people honours me with their lips, but their hearts are far from me; in vain do they worship me, teaching human precepts as doctrines.'

Now, of course, God is not against singing. He loves music. He inspired the greatest songbook ever composed, the Psalms. He ordered huge numbers of musicians to be trained to play at festivals in the temple in Jerusalem. God's not against music. He's against hypocrisy.

The problem with the people of Amos's day was that they sang joyful songs to God on the sabbath, and ripped off their neighbours and oppressed the poor for the rest of the week. So Amos pointed out that real worship would happen when they 'let justice roll down like waters, and righteousness like an everflowing stream'. All too often we need to hear the same message.

Amos 5:24

Romans 12:1–2

Paul says: 'Present your bodies as a living sacrifice, holy and acceptable to God, which is your spiritual worship. Do not be conformed to this world, but be transformed by the renewing of your minds.' In other words, as we've already said, real worship is a matter of lifestyle.

For this reason it is very unhelpful when people in church or at meetings say, 'We will now move into a time of worship.' It suggests that what we were doing before was not worship. It implies that there is a division between our lives with God and our lives in the world – a division which is both unhelpful and unbiblical.

What we do in church on Sundays and in our other gatherings is simply to change the mode or style of our worship from (for instance) work to singing, from washing up to breaking bread. Everything we do is an act of worship. In the classic *The Practice of the Presence of God* it is said that the foundation of Brother Lawrence's spiritual life 'had been a lofty idea and conception of God by faith. Once he had firmly grasped this, he had no other care than to cast faithfully aside from the beginning every other thought, so as to do all that he did for the love of God.' That is worship as lifestyle.

Brother Lawrence, *The Practice of the Presence of God* (Hodder and Stoughton), p. 26.

*t*ouching the throne

Having said all that, and keeping it firmly in our minds, for most of us worship *is* what we do in church, or when we're on our own 'just praisin' the Lord'. This is the common usage of the word, so that is how we will use it in the remainder of this chapter. The point of what we've said so far is that such worship must reflect our daily lives, as well as focus our attention on the lofty grandeur of God.

". . . just praisin' the Lord . . ."

That being so, what we say and sing in church must be rooted in the real world in which we live. The trouble with so much worship is that it is other-worldly, divorced from daily reality, devoid of meaning for office workers and factory hands. It neither reflects our real lives (putting into words how

Read Isaiah 40:12–31

we feel) nor focuses our thinking on the God who creates, sustains, renews and empowers the world and his people. This is true of both old hymns and new songs. It is probably at the heart of so much disquiet, grumbling and complaining about worship.

'I feel such a hypocrite sometimes,' Jill confessed. 'I say to myself, "You can't sing that after what you've been doing this week." '

'I often stop singing,' chipped in Norman with a grin, 'and ask myself, "What is this song about?" We sing so much tripe.'

'What I need every week is something that is going to shift my attention from myself and place it squarely back on God,' said Grace.

Psalm 122:1

'Yes,' Paul agreed. 'I need to hear God's voice clearly. I need feeding on Sunday with something nourishing enough to last the week.'

'I often come to church and feel that everyone else is on cloud nine,' said Ron. 'It's only me who's having trouble at work, a struggle with sin or doubts about God.'

All these good, faithful Christians illustrate a major problem about Sunday worship: it has to cater for such a wide variety of needs and aspirations, preferences and prejudices. What so often happens is that it reflects only the mood of the worship leader.

One from the heart

'If he plays this much more slowly, this hymn's going to last till the second coming,' I mumbled to myself as we dragged our way interminably through *Sing We the King who is Coming to Reign*. I stopped trying to sing, and listened. It was horrible; people all around me were singing at different speeds, some in different keys, few smiling. 'This is ridiculous,' I thought. 'I can't worship here.'

On another occasion I began to be very aware of the ache in my legs because I'd been standing for so long. We began *Jesus, Holy and Anointed One* for what seemed like the hundredth time. When it finally came to an end, everyone carried on making a noise, some repeating 'Jesus' over and over again, and some speaking in tongues under their breath but loud enough for those around them to hear. Others, with hands raised, kept saying 'Yes' (just like the TSB). Someone suddenly announced: 'We'll all pray for the local council.'

'Oh, good,' I said to myself. Barely were the words formed in my mind before my ears were assaulted by everyone praying at once at the top of their voices. It was incoherent. 'What a din!' I thought. 'It's like the tower of Babel. I can't worship here.'

We've all had experiences like those, I'm sure. We've felt really out of place and unable to worship. We focus on the style, decide 'I can't worship that way,' and shut off. Worse, we focus on ourselves and say, 'I'm not getting anything out of this.' So we feel let down, disillusioned, robbed of experiencing the nearness of God.

But we are robbing ourselves by choosing to opt out. Surely it is better to find something in what is happening that can provide a focus for our thinking and praying, and concentrate on that rather than on what's going on around us. 'Accentuate the positive', even in the midst of the negative. The

"... speaking in tongues under their breath..."

"What can God have that gives him greater satisfaction than that a thousand thousand times a day all his creatures should pause to worship him in the heart?"
Brother Lawrence

worst worship surely contains enough about God to stimulate our own reflection and devotion, even if we feel we can't sing the songs.

'Everything at Greenbelt is worship,' enthused one youthful participant. That worship is very different from what happens Sunday by Sunday at Westminster Chapel or Westminster Abbey or yearly at Spring Harvest.

'Different' does not mean 'better' or 'worse'. Styles differ, but no one style is more authentic or real or 'spiritual' as worship than another. There is no 'right' style of worship. All worship is cultural, and therefore style is a matter of preference. Some prefer hymns to choruses, spontaneity to liturgy, long sermons to lots of singing. There is no God-given way of going about it.

Mercifully, the Bible says very little about *how* to worship (whatever the plethora of 'how to' manuals published in the last decade would have us believe). The Bible stresses that it is the *content* of worship – whom we worship and what we declare about him – that matters. The style is up to individual worshippers.

E.g. *Deuteronomy 6:4–6*

What tends to happen is that churches adopt a sort of cultural fascism with regard to worship. 'This is the way we do it here,' is heard up and down the land, from trad Baptist, through trendy Anglican, to off-the-wall house church. We all think that we've alighted on *the* way to worship, as if we had discovered some holy grail.

" . . . a sort of cultural fascism with regard to worship . . ."

The truth is, there are lots of ways to worship. Our lives, both personal and corporate, would be greatly enriched by trying a

ONCE MORE, WITH FEELING

few of the ways we don't normally follow in our church.

*i*t takes all colours to make a rainbow

Because worship is about the whole of life, its Sunday expression should reflect the whole gamut of human creativity. So worship is a place for dance, drama, poetry, storytelling, songs, instrumental music, liturgies, visual art, slide and film, candles, flowers, banners, beautiful furniture, freedom, order, listening, participating, sitting, standing, kneeling, lying down (though not necessarily all at once!).

See Psalm 150

The problem is, most of us are not in a position to influence the style of worship in our church. That is set by ministers, worship groups and organists. But one way of exploring the landscape of worship is to spend time on our own, worshipping the Lord in a way we haven't tried before.

This is most easily done through books and tapes. Here are a few ideas.

There are a lot of worship tapes on the market. If your church and worship experience is broadly charismatic – *Songs of Fellowship*, *Songs of the Vineyard* – try to get hold of worship material from the Iona Community, Taizé, or somewhere else with a very different tradition or style from the one you are used to. Iona material, for instance (sung unaccompanied by the Wild Goose Worship Group, often to traditional Scottish or African tunes), focuses a lot on meeting God in the ordinary things of life.

If your experience of worship music is

"... meeting God in the ordinary things of life ..."

mainly hymns, then dip into tapes by musicians such as Graham Kendrick, Dave Bilborough and Chris Bowater, many of whose songs are rich in good Christian teaching and biblical response to God.

Other Christian tapes can enhance worship. I find some of Bruce Cockburn's music, for instance, a challenge to my view of God and his world. For example:

> Moment of peace like brief Arctic bloom
> Red/gold ripple of sun going down
> Line of black hills makes my bed
> Sky full of love pulled over my head
> World of wonders . . .

Or

> Somebody touched me
> Like the rain in the wind
> Left me alone
> Feeling like I'd been skinned.
> But I know you're with me
> Whatever I go through
> Somebody touched me
> I know it was you.

Randy Stonehill is another whose vision of the world and of the Christian life is an aid to my worship.

> Though you hold all creation
> In your holy hands
> Though the world is as weightless
> As a grain of sand
> Still you told me my name
> Gave me strength to stand
> O my Lord.

Listening to an album of this quality can be a most rewarding worship experience. At the end of it I feel closer to God, and I've had my vision sharpened and my ears and eyes sensitized to what God is up to around me. Why don't you try it?

Among the books that are worth giving a try are *Daily with God* (which is good for quiet times). It is a selection of readings and prayers for every day of the year which focus the mind on God and put our response into words that the church has used for centuries.

One of the very useful things about set prayers and liturgies is that they teach us how to pray. They show us new ways of constructing our prayers, and open up a whole new landscape of subjects that we can pray about. By voicing prayers in a way that we would probably never have thought of, they frequently enlarge our vision of God and his involvement in our world.

"... a whole new landscape of subjects ..."

Charlotte, our elder daughter, has a book of first prayers that she is currently reading at bedtime. It is helping her to extend the range of her praying, from thanking God for her nice day and asking for a good night's sleep, to praying for the sick, for forgiveness, that God would help her work hard and be obedient – things she might not have thought of, left to herself.

Particularly if you belong to one of the new churches, or are used to worship that is very contemporary, such resources can broaden and deepen your worship of God. It can help us tap into the rich heritage of Christian worship. Ours is not the first generation to discover the wonder of adoring and praising God, so let's learn from those who've gone before.

Another way of opening doors to new

"Forms and rituals do not produce worship, nor does the formal disuse of forms and rituals."
Richard Foster

styles of worship is to talk to other people. What do they like? What helps them to focus on God? What helps them voice their praise, adoration and gratitude to God? Would what works for them, work for you?

***m*aking sweet music together**

It cannot be denied that over the past twenty years there has been an explosion of new worship songs and song-writers. Some of it is very good. Some of it is appalling. As Paul Wigmore says, often we are 'being offered ephemeral flotsam for the worship of the eternal Godhead, the ridiculous for the expression of the sublime'.

With the wealth of new material available, it is hard to know what to pick for congregations to sing Sunday by Sunday. But might I enter a plea here for the triumph of content over style? It doesn't matter that a particular song rocks the worship leader's socks off, if the words are gibberish. It is a sad fact that there is too much material around that is theologically illiterate as well as poetically trite and musically banal. The latter two faults are excusable – some Christian music was ever thus – but the first is unacceptable and dangerous.

See Colossians 3:16–17

For the new generation of Christians growing to maturity, much of their understanding of the faith is being formed, not by preaching or reading, but by worship songs. This would be all right if the church were still producing writers of the calibre of Charles Wesley and Isaac Watts. But, with a few notable exceptions, all we are producing are

Read Romans 10:17

writers of the quality of teenyboppers' pop idols.

We need to pay careful attention to the content of what we sing. When we worship, the focus should be on God. Too many songs these days talk about 'how I feel', while very few actually talk about God, his character and attributes. Even those that are about God major on what he's done for *me*, and so the focus comes back to the worshipper.

For this reason it would be good to see a shift away from worship services dominated by singing, to services that have more of a mix of praying, reading, listening and music. Worship should recall the mighty deeds of God through reading Scripture, using drama and, of course, preaching. It should draw our focus away from the smallness of our world and day-to-day concerns, and on to the glorious vastness of God. Sunday by Sunday, we need to glimpse afresh the majestic holiness and awesome otherness of God. If we are to be sustained through the week by our faith in God, then we must be helped to appreciate that he is big enough to trust.

The Bible speaks of 'magnifying' the Lord through our worship. It is not that we make him bigger, of course, but that in our worship our vision of him is enlarged. He fills more of our conscious minds; he forms a greater part of our thinking and feeling.

"We should feed our soul with a lofty conception of God and from that derive great joy in being his."
Brother Lawrence

E.g. *Psalm 34:3*

As we focus our attention on him, he takes his rightful place at the centre of our lives, and all rivals to his authority are unseated and banished. Worship that propels us into the heavenlies to gaze on the glory of our God is vital if we are going to serve that God through the week at work and home.

". . . the emotional buzz we get from a good tune .."

Too much focus on myself, my feelings, my needs and my fears, does nothing to feed my faith. The content of worship material needs to shift the focus of our attention away from ourselves squarely on to God. We must never confuse the emotional buzz we get from a good tune, with a touch from God.

Actions speak louder than words

Worship is the submission of all our nature to God [said William Temple, Archbishop of Canterbury before the war]. It is the quickening of conscience by his holiness; the nourishment of mind with his truth; the purifying of imagination by his beauty; the opening of the heart to his love; the surrender of will to his purpose – all that gathered up in adoration, the most selfless emotion of which our nature is capable and therefore the chief remedy for that self-centredness which is our original sin and the source of all actual sin.

That long quotation is worth pondering and chewing over. It is the best definition of worship that I've found. It stresses that worship is a lifestyle, a conscious placing of ourselves on the altar before God, a giving of ourselves completely to the service of God.

It makes two vital truths abundantly clear. First, the lifestyle of worship he speaks of will be fed by quality Sunday worship with its emphasis on content – drawing people's whole attention to the glorious God we serve – and variety.

Secondly, it stresses that good Sunday worship depends on good Monday and Tuesday and Wednesday and Thursday and Friday and Saturday worship. Good singing, praying and listening worship depends on a humble walk with God that seeks to do justice and love mercy. Good liturgy is fed by a godly lifestyle.

> One of the scribes . . . asked him: 'Which commandment is the first of all?' Jesus answered, 'The first is, "Hear, O Israel: the Lord our God, the Lord is one; you shall love the Lord your God with all your heart, and with all your soul, and with all your mind, and with all your strength." '

Mark 12:28–30

*a*ny good books?

The best I've read are Barry Liesch, *People in the Presence of God* (Highland); Graham Kendrick, *Worship* (Kingsway); Eleanor Kreider, *Enter his Gates* (Marshall Pickering); and Paul Beasley-Murray, *Faith and Festivity* (Marc) – this last book is a guide for worship leaders, but ought to be more widely read. There's a good-ish chapter on worship in Richard Foster, *Celebration of Discipline* (Hodder and Stoughton).

Two short works have exercised a considerable influence on my understanding of worship: C. F. D. Moule, *Worship in the New Testament* (Grove Liturgical Study, 12: Grove Books), and Howard Marshall, 'How

Far did the Early Christians Worship God?' in *Churchman*, 99, 1985. Also helpful here is Robert Banks, *Paul's Idea of Community* (Paternoster).

Good collections of worship materials for use either alone or in groups, including church on Sundays, include John de Gruchy, *Cry Justice: Prayers, Meditations and Readings from South Africa* (Collins); John Pitchford, *Daily with God* (Canterbury Press); and Michael Perry, Patrick Goodland and Angela Griffiths, *Prayers for the People* (Marshall Pickering).

Brother Lawrence, *The Practice of the Presence of God*, is excellent. It is published by Hodder and Stoughton in their *Christian Classics* series.

The music referred to in this chapter is Bruce Cockburn's 'World of Wonders' on the album of the same name; his 'Somebody Touched Me' on the album *Nothing But a Burning Light*; and Randy Stonehill's 'When I Look to the Mountains' from the album *Celebrate this Heartbeat*.

THERE ARE MORE QUESTIONS THAN ANSWERS

C H A P T E R

The Dayglo orange poster shouted its message from the peeling notice-board in the churchyard: 'Jesus is the answer. What's your question?'

As a young Christian I thought this was a pretty silly slogan. After all, the answer to the question 'Where do I catch the 27 bus?' is not 'Jesus'. But as I grew older and a little wiser, I came to see that it was a more fundamentally silly slogan than my first impression told me.

Its silliness lies not in the statement itself but in the attitude behind it. It is an attitude that says life is simple, its problems are easily solved, and its questions have straightforward answers. If you believe, everything will be OK.

And that isn't so, is it?

'I'm sure that God must be displeased with me because of all these doubts,' Joan said. 'We should have faith, I know, but I can't all the time. I keep wanting to know why.'

'We should never question God, I know. But I have to,' declared Bill. 'All the things that have happened recently have rocked us and shaken our faith. They've forced us to ask, "What's going on?" '

I know how these good people feel. So does the writer of Psalm 73, which will occupy us for most of this chapter. And all four of us are in the dark. There are more questions than answers. There's more going on in the world than we can ever grasp, or fit into our tidy understanding of life, the universe and everything. And it is no help to any of us when well-meaning Christians say, 'Don't worry. Just believe. It'll be OK.'

". . . our tidy understanding of life . . ."

$a$sk me another

Geraldine came to see me. She's been a Christian for quite a while. In her life she has struggled with depression, the problems of poor housing and lack of work, and the difficulties of raising a family. She has been assailed by doubts. But worse, she has been afflicted by Christians who have offered simple solutions to the problems with which she wrestles.

'I was told the other day that I should be delivered from these doubts I have, and that I must have an evil spirit in me that causes me to doubt,' she said. She spoke quite calmly, but she had spent the night in tears. The words of a well-meaning Christian had branded her a failure with a deficient faith. She looked me full in the face. 'Do you think I'm wicked for thinking these things?'

Os Guinness tells a story about seeing a peasant with a loaded donkey. The donkey wasn't moving, so the peasant shouted at it. The donkey collapsed, so the peasant beat it and beat it. So many Christians are like that, Guinness observed. They demand of themselves that they believe this and agree with that, and that they have more faith and stop doubting.

"The donkey collapsed, so the peasant beat it . . ."

His observation is a wise one. To it I would add that Christians are intolerant of other Christians who doubt. And so, like the peasant with his donkey, we beat one another with our words. In effect, we say to our doubting friend: 'Your faith isn't worth much if you have so many doubts. You are letting the side down, and doing the devil's work by not having faith.'

I suspect the reason for this stems from our own inability to handle doubt and uncertainty. If other people keep raising questions about what they feel to be the inadequacy of their faith, we begin to sense that our own faith is under attack. Instead of resolving others' doubt, we shut it out by labelling them defective in their faith. That way, we don't have to face the same questions rising in our own hearts.

Doubt causes a great deal of fear in Christians. This is due to a misunderstanding of what doubt really is. We so often see doubt as unbelief, the opposite of faith, and hence as sinful. After all, Jesus said that the world's sin was unbelief. So doubt must be some-

John 16:9

"Doubt is not the same as unbelief."

thing that we are supposed to repent of.

But this is a misunderstanding. Doubt is not the same as unbelief. Doubt, as Os Guinness helpfully described it, is faith in two minds. Doubt is the questions we ask about our faith. Doubt is what we feel when there is a gap between what we believe and what we experience, between what we say and sing in church and what happens to us in the world.

This was the dilemma of the poet who wrote Psalm 73. It is a wonderful psalm, full of honesty and faith, which looks the real world squarely in the eye and affirms that there are reasons to believe, even when life is tough. If it is handled properly, doubt is not the doorway to unbelief, but the midwife of a deeper, stronger, more resilient and realistic faith.

*t*he reality gap

The poet begins by quoting a creed, a statement of faith, that he'd no doubt recited many times in the temple. It had a hollow ring: 'Truly God is good to the upright, to those who are pure in heart.' This is the same kind of statement as 'Jesus is the answer. What's your question?' Superficially, it looks true and very spiritual. But fundamentally it does not address life in the real world.

Psalm 73:1

The Bible is full of people who challenge the nice, religious things we say with questions like:

- 'Yes, but does it really work?' (Ecclesiastes)
- 'I hear what you're saying, but how do I know it's true?' (Thomas)

Eccles. 1:13–14, 17–18; 2:12–17; etc.
John 20:24–29

- 'How come you gave me such a rotten job, Lord?' (Jeremiah)
- 'No, surely that's not the way?' (Peter)

Even when the disciples received the Great Commission from the visibly risen Jesus, Matthew tells us, 'some doubted'.

Jeremiah 11:18–23; 12:1–6; 15:10–21; 17:14–18; 18:18–23; 20:7–18 Matthew 16:21–23; 28:17

The biblical tradition is one of expressing doubts honestly and fully to God. We find this rather uncomfortable because of our appetite for stories of success and triumph, testimonies of how God made someone's life wonderful beyond our wildest dreams. Such books top the Christian bestseller lists. But, as Eugene Peterson points out, 'the stories are not honest'. It is not that their authors are lying, or making up the stories they tell. Rather, it is that they leave out the hard bits, the times of doubt, uncertainty, questioning and darkness.

Eugene H. Peterson, *Five Smooth Stones for Pastoral Work* (Eerdmans/ Gracewing), p. 51.

Such books lead us ordinary Christian readers (who do not experience a miracle a day before breakfast) to assume that there's something wrong with our lives, and that somehow we are not living by faith the way these authors seem to be. We become dispirited and guilty.

It was stories like these that led the poet of Psalm 73 to ask what faith was all about. He'd heard such stories, and even recited statements of faith based on them in church. Yet his life was not great. Worse than that, when he looked at the world it was the pagans who were getting blessed, not the believers.

Hence he describes himself as stumbling, slipping, tottering, reeling. The pagans had it all. They were healthy and tanned, proud, greedy and uncaring. They didn't believe in

Psalm 73:2–16

"Why bother to be holy?"

God, yet they had no troubles; they lived lives of ease without a care in the world. Believers, on the other hand (well, let's be honest here, this particular believer), were plagued by troubles and difficulties.

It caused him to doubt God and the value of being a believer at all. 'All in vain I have kept my heart clean', he protests, 'and washed my hands in innocence.' In other words, why bother to be holy, to strive to live a life of faith, when all I get is troubles; and the pagan, who doesn't give a fig for God, is living in the lap of untroubled luxury?

I suspect that if we voiced such things in our churches, we'd be taken on one side for counselling. In some churches we'd be delivered of a spirit of unbelief. In others, we'd be told that we couldn't teach Sunday school because there were doubts about our soundness. What I find so sobering and so encouraging is that the people who compiled the book of Psalms, under the guidance of the Holy Spirit, as the hymbook for the people of Israel when they came back from exile, wanted to sing this psalm in the temple. What a contrast!

*I*n France they kiss on Main Street

Canadian singer Joni Mitchell kicks off her album *The Hissing of Summer Lawns* with the bright and breezy 'In France They Kiss on Main Street', which contrasts the rather inhibited North American attitude to lovers kissing in public with the Gallic *joie de vivre* which thinks nothing of embracing a loved one at the bus stop or at a pedestrian crossing in the Place du Concord.

It's not cheap display, the singer protests, but the freedom to be yourself. That may or may not be the case with respect to kissing in public. But it could be the case with respect to airing our doubts in public. It is one thing to be honest with doubts, rigorous in asking questions. It is quite another to flaunt our doubts, as the French, according to Mitchell, flaunt their kisses – 'like bright flags hung on holidays'.

The psalmist recognizes this danger. 'If I had said, "I will talk on in this way," I would have been untrue to the circle of your children.'

Psalm 73:15

The problem, of course, is to achieve a balance. It is right to air our doubts, difficulties and problems with individuals and in small groups where we are known and loved. It is probably not helpful to announce a crisis of faith just as the preacher is standing to deliver a sermon to a packed church on Sunday morning.

The reason it is appropriate to say or sing Psalm 73 in church on Sundays is that, by virtue of *everyone* saying or singing it, it becomes a general statement of the kind of doubts all Christians have from time to time. If an individual rose in church to speak of a similar questioning of faith, it would at best be embarrassing for all concerned. At worst, it could lead other, younger, less secure Christians to doubt and question certainties with which they previously had no difficulty.

So the psalmist is sensitive as to where he asks his questions and shares his doubts, for fear of unsettling the faith of others – especially those younger and less established in the faith than he. I generally avoid visiting elderly people in winter if I feel a cold or 'flu coming on, just in case I pass my infection on to them. A forty-eight-hour 'flu to me could spell two weeks in hospital for someone older and less able to fight infection. So it is with doubt. Be honest about your doubts to God and to close friends. Don't flaunt them in front of everyone.

"Be honest about your doubts to God . . ."

getting the issues into focus

'I just can't think straight about this at all,' James said nervously, pulling at his fingertips and crossing his legs. 'There are so many issues, all bound up together: issues about my involvement in church, my work life, a particular relationship and where I should live. It's a mess.' He laughed. 'It sounds a great scenario for a sitcom, doesn't it? But it's not funny really.'

His problem is a common one. Our doubts are rarely single-issue affairs. Sometimes we doubt a specific doctrine of the church, such as the virgin birth or the bodily resurrection of Jesus. Sometimes our doubts are bound up with an issue of guidance: we don't know which way to go, and praying doesn't seem much help. More often than not, our doubts and questions are triggered by things that happen to us, and are both intellectual and emotional.

Michael, for instance, came to see me with doubts about the power of God. 'The Bible claims that God is powerful and answers prayer,' he complained. 'You know, "Where two or three are gathered . . ." So how come

God doesn't answer?'

'What have you asked for?' I ventured gently.

'Oh, I'm seeking guidance for the future. I want to be certain I'm doing the right thing. I want to experience more of God in my life; I want to get more out of church on Sunday; I want my girlfriend to come to know the Lord . . .'

I cut in at that point, before he got on to wanting all diseases in the world to be cured, all wars to cease, a solution to unemployment, and all the homeless housed. His doubts about the ability of God to answer prayer had more to do with impatience than with unbelief. He wanted certainty, direction, solutions, power and ecstasy, and he wanted them all *now*. 'Hold on,' I interrupted. 'Rome wasn't built in a day. Let's separate the issues and tackle them one by one. But let's remember that the Christian life is a journey of discovery. We are not given a blueprint at the beginning, which answers all our questions and charts our course in intimate detail.'

"We are not given a blueprint . . ."

The poet in Psalm 73 wrestled with the issues and concluded that there were more questions than answers. But, along the way, the fundamental issue that lies at the root of all the other issues came into focus. Why do I believe? Am I in this for what I can get out of it, or because knowing God is better than anything else? It's the question confronted by Shadrach, Meshach and Abednego as they faced the fiery furnace. 'If our God whom we serve is able to deliver us from the furnace of blazing fire . . . let him deliver us. But if not, . . . we will [still] not serve your gods.'

Psalm 73:16

Daniel 3:16–18

In other words, we believe in God because

God is worth knowing. If he does good things for us, that's a bonus. It is not the reason we believe. This is the position the psalmist was coming to, and the rest of the psalm shows us how he got there.

*I*n the beginning and in the end . . . GOD

Psalm 73:17

Working with doubt in order to come to a deeper faith begins with seeing the heart of the matter. At the centre of the psalm, as at the centre of the universe, is God. And the psalmist saw it. How? Well, it happened in the temple. So, possibly, it was as a result of worship, or of hearing the Scriptures read or a sermon preached. It could happen to us in the same way, perhaps as we dwell on the central drama of our faith at a communion service.

The psalmist did not only get God back into focus. He also got the world back into focus too. For, as he saw God, so he saw the future of the carefree pagan. And that future was none too pleasant.

". . . the future of the carefree pagan . . ."

Psalm 73:21–26

Having stumbled at the start, he is now standing. But his seeking and searching are not over. The key section of the psalm, dealing with how we resolve the conflict between faith and experience, between what we say in church and what we see in the world, is just beginning.

The fact that God had come into focus doesn't mean that everything was now handed to the poet on a plate. He'd been like an animal, he confesses, because he had just reacted instinctively to things he saw in the world and to words he heard and said in church. Now he begins to think about those things. How can I make sense of what I know to be true of God and what I see in the world? Resolving doubt is a process – sometimes a long one. It is not a case of shutting our eyes and saying, 'I've seen all I need to. I believe now.'

The first thing the psalmist did was to *pray*. From verse 17 he starts to speak to God. Up to then, he had been talking about his experience, what he's seen, and what he's heard of God. Now he speaks to God.

The Psalms are a great encouragement to us to say what is on our hearts. In the Psalms we find the people of God voicing their complaints and anger, their pain and sorrow, their hate and fear, their doubts and questions to God.

'My God, my God, why have you forsaken me?'

'My soul thirsts for God . . . when shall I come and behold the face of God?'

'My soul also is struck with terror, while you, O Lord – how long?'

Psalms 22:1; 42:2; 6:3

Resolving doubt and difficulties begins by honestly telling God all about it. We get no heavenly Brownie points for bottling it all up and pretending to God that everything is hunky-dory. Jesus urged us to pray honestly, because our Father knows what's going on before we tell him.

Matthew 7:7–13

The second thing the psalmist did was to *go to the Scriptures*. He speaks of God guiding him with his counsel. As we have seen, the Bible needs to be read as a story and as a collection of stories. The problem that this psalm starts with is the problem of a faulty approach to Scripture.

We read that God is good to his people. We define 'good' to mean that God will give us everything we want because he loves us. We decide what we want and ask for it. After all, Jesus said to ask for whatever we want in his name, and we'll get it. When we don't get what we wanted, we begin to doubt God.

What we should doubt is our use of Scripture, which at times reduces God to a slot machine into which we insert our coins in order to get chocolate or fizzy pop.

When we read Scripture, we need to read it as a whole, enter into the struggles, and hear what the Spirit is saying about God and his people as we read. Tackle books like Esther, Job and Revelation as well as the gospels and the letters of Paul. God's counsel is the entire story from Genesis to Revelation, not just the edited highlights we find on calendars.

Psalm 73:25

Thirdly, the poet *weighed the alternatives*. 'Whom have I in heaven but you? And there is nothing on earth that I desire other than you.' It is important to recognize that doubt has an intellectual element. Some of the questions we ask have to do with whether the world makes sense. Is there a God, and, if so, what is he like? What is our purpose on earth? Does anyone or anything, other than the God revealed in the Bible and in Jesus Christ, make sense of the life we lead?

Read John 6:68

For the poet, the answer was a resounding 'No'. Nothing in the surrounding religions and philosophies drew him. He knew that the answer lay with God and the Bible, and therefore he would stay and wrestle with the questions until he resolved his doubt. Some of our questions await answers that we will only get in heaven.

Fourthly, the poet *looked to the future*. Having weighed the alternatives to God, it's as well to bear in mind that one of the greatest puzzles in life is what happens to us when we die. We live for seventy or eighty years, which isn't very long. What happens for the rest of eternity? The poet saw the destiny of the pagan and the destiny of the believer, and concluded that, despite the number of questions he had outstanding, sticking with God was a better long-term bet than throwing in his lot with the non-believer.

Psalm 73:17–20

We are often racked by doubt because we lack an eternal perspective. Our culture is bound up with, and preoccupied with, the 'now'. Its obsession with health and fitness, entertainment and leisure, creature comforts and domestic appliances, is all to ensure that life now is wonderful and fulfilling because all that comes after it is old age and death. The Bible, however, cautions us to view this life in the light of the life to come, because the latter is infinitely longer than the former.

". . . sticking with God was a better long-term bet . . ."

Finally, the poet *looked for God in the current situation*. Even in the darkness, God is there. Instead of throwing up our hands in horror when things don't work out as we expected, and declaring that Christianity is no good, we should sit down and wonder, 'What is God saying to me? Where is he taking me? Why is he leading me this way?

Psalm 139:7–12

*h*e put my feet on firmer ground

At the end of his poem, this brave, intelligent writer came to a surer faith. It was no longer

"... it is better to be in the dark with God than anywhere else without him ..."

Psalm 46:1

a faith grounded on what he could get out of it. It was a faith built on God himself.

Doubt is resolved when we can say, 'But for me it is good to be near God.' This is the opposite of the consumer faith with which he started – the kind of faith that constantly asks, 'What's in this for me?' In its place, the poet had come to a pure, unshakeable faith that rests in God alone, and not in what God gives us or does for us or has in store for us – marvellous and wonderful though those things are.

It is a faith that knows God as a refuge. We need a refuge, a shelter, only when we know that storms are coming. If we think the life of faith is all plain sailing ('Sign on the dotted line and hop aboard for the smooth ride to heaven'), then we don't need a refuge. But that's not biblical faith. The Bible knows only the fierce faith of pilgrims in the storm – be that sickness, doubt, or economic hardship – for whom God is their refuge, their fortress, their very present help in trouble.

At the end of the poem, the writer had not had all his questions answered. Indeed, he might not have had any of them answered fully. There will always be more questions than answers in this life. But he had wrestled with those questions and doubts honestly before God, and had come through to a deeper, simpler faith that knows that it is better to be in the dark with God than anywhere else without him.

I'll leave the last word to two brothers wiser than I. 'Faith', says Philip Yancey, 'means believing in advance what will only make sense in reverse.' And Eugene Peterson reminds us that 'the person who

Philip Yancey, *Seeing in the Dark* (Marshall Pickering), p. 201.

responds to the saving event of God in Christ does not feel continuously and without the disturbances of doubt oneness with God, although he or she knows that all sins are forgiven.'

Eugene H. Peterson, *Five Smooth Stones for Pastoral Work*, p. 49.

*S*ome helpful books

There are a number of excellent books on this subject. I'll mention the two I have found most helpful. In the States, Philip Yancey's book *Seeing in the Dark* (Marshall Pickering) has the infinitely better title *Disappointment with God*; why the British publisher had to change it I'll never know. Robert Davidson, *The Courage to Doubt* (SCM) is a study of leading Old Testament people's struggles with doubt. It is not for the fainthearted, but it is a glorious and faith-affirming read.

Os Guinness, *Doubt: Faith in Two Minds* (Lion) is very good, if heavy going. Alister McGrath, *Doubt: Handling it Honestly* (IVP) is less daunting but still very helpful.

Russ Parker, *Free to Fail* (Triangle) shows how to cope with failure in our lives and use it for good. It's worth the price just for the chapter on the cross – 'Christ and a Cross for Failures'.

The Eugene Peterson references in this chapter are from his book *Five Smooth Stones for Pastoral Work* (Eerdmans/Gracewing), a look at the pastoral use of five Old Testament books. It's a compelling and helpful, though demanding, read.

And, of course, the very best book on doubt is the Bible – especially Job, Ecclesiastes, the Psalms, the gospels and Revelation.

I DON'T KNOW WHICH
WAY TO TURN

5

C   H   A   P   T   E   R

'But there are a lot of people who just will not understand why you are taking this course of action at this time.' I tried to sound calm as I struggled to get a handle on what I was hearing. After a good half an hour, I was flummoxed. I felt as though I was drowning in a sea of words and flailing about for some driftwood of meaning, but none was floating anywhere near me.

'God gave us a verse this morning and that clinched it,' Jerry stated, bright as a button. His face told me that what he was saying was perfectly reasonable to him, so what was my problem?

I wanted to say that the verse in question had nothing to do with the issue under discussion – namely, whether Jerry should team up with a different church and launch a project to help the homeless. Come to think of it, it had nothing to say about choosing a spouse, changing a job, or global nuclear disarmament, either. As far as I could tell, the verse was about the persecution that could well arise from our Christian commitment. I wouldn't base a lifestyle choice on it – certainly not one as important as leaving a fellowship and taking a leap of faith that would give Moses pause for thought.

". . . a leap of faith that would give Moses pause for thought . . ."

But guidance is so often like that. It comes across as a deep conviction that God has prompted a particular course of action and confirmed it from his Word. Only a sceptic would raise an objection. You can't argue with 'God told me to do it'. Well, you're not meant to.

But just suppose that God doesn't guide people in this way. Just suppose that God expects the decisions we make to be open to reasonable enquiry and rational scrutiny. What would guidance look like then?

'How am I meant to make up my mind?' demanded Monica, agitated by the complete sense of hopelessness she was feeling. 'I mean, it looks a good job and I think I'm qualified for it. But I don't feel God telling me to do it. At the back of my mind is the thought that I'm doing it for the money, and because I've got no endurance to stick at this job that I hate, and that I'm in danger of stepping out of God's will.'

She is not alone in her dilemma. So many Christians find themselves paralysed by uncertainty when it comes to making decisions that those with no faith make every day with apparently little or no trouble. 'I don't know which way to turn' is a common cry.

*m*ama told me not to come

As children we have precious little choice. Our parents make most decisions for us: what we eat, where we live, what we wear, where we go to school. As we grow up we start to decide more things for ourselves: which children to play with, what TV programmes to watch, which food to like. Part of growing up is about learning to make good decisions and sensible choices. Part of being a parent is teaching a child to make those decisions.

Being a Christian ought to be the same. But it doesn't seem to work that way. Somewhere down the line we take on board the strong notion that every decision we make must be based on a direct lead from the Lord.

One of the wisest, brightest Christians I knew was Hugh Sylvester, the rector of Holy Trinity, Platt, in Manchester. I was talking to him one day about a job I was applying for, and was just coming round to asking him for a reference when he remarked: 'Simon, you know this job isn't worth doing. And if it were, you'd be the last person suited to do it!'

I was more than a little crushed. Over the previous few days, as I'd filled in the application form and talked to the person who might have been my boss, I'd begun to feel that this was for me. It was a job with a

"But it doesn't seem to work that way."

Christian organization, using my communication skills, working closely with other people, and doing some apologetic-style evangelism. It was heaven sent.

'The trouble with it', Hugh continued, noting my crestfallen expression out of the corner of his eye, 'is that it will give you no useful skills. What you need to do is learn a trade, and to get a feel for living in the world, managing money, shopping, running a home. You've lived a pretty cosseted life as a student. Get out into the real world.'

I couldn't contain myself any longer. 'But I think God wants me to do it,' I blurted out indignantly. 'I've prayed and I feel good about it.' That, I assumed, would be the clincher.

'Simon, some time ago I was asked to take on another role in the diocese. So I prayed about it and thought about it, and asked God whether I should do it. Do you know what he said?'

I was on the edge of my seat. I'd only had *feelings* that God had approved, but Hugh had had a word from the Lord.

'God said, "You make up your mind, you're growing up." '

That was not what I had wanted to hear. But it was the best piece of advice I've ever received on the subject of guidance.

"You make up your mind, you're growing up."

*h*ow did I get into this mess?

A lot later, years after following Hugh's advice and getting myself a trade (financial journalism), and years after his untimely death, I put his advice into effect again. I had been offered a job in a different, though related, field. I weighed up the options. Could I do the work? Was the work worth doing? Would I enjoy it as much as, or more than, what I was doing already? Did I want to leave my current colleagues? How would it affect my home life? What kind of prospects did it have? Would it help me realize my goals in life?

I talked to a close friend about it. I prayed with Linda and my home group. Someone had a picture, a word: balloons rising over the City of London and bursting. (I was a bit nonplussed by that!)

I took the job. Three months later I left. It was a disaster! (Maybe that's what the bursting balloons were about.)

If it had happened years before, I would have felt not only a failure in work terms, but also guilty. I would have felt that I must have disobeyed God; how else could I have ended up in this mess? I was sorry it hadn't worked out. Perhaps I should have taken more notice of the picture. And, of course, I needed to find something else pronto. But I didn't feel guilty.

I told this story to Dave, who was deeply troubled over a decision that he had to make. 'I would have been wrecked by that experience,' he confessed. 'I'd feel a failure, and assume that everyone in the church thought I was a failure. But worse, I'd feel that I must have disobeyed God and that I was in real trouble.'

'I would have felt that once,' I confided, 'but I believe God wants us to make wise decisions and take responsibility for our lives. If we get it wrong, then God's in the

". . . balloons rising over the City of London and bursting . . ."

See Ephesians 5:15–16

81

redemption business – he can work to redeem and bring good out of even my worst decisions, providing, of course, I'm open to him. He certainly brought good things out of that disaster.'

One step backwards but two in the right direction

'I was unhappy and unsure if I should continue going to my church.' Ann, brought up as a Catholic, was feeling increasingly uneasy about her particular priest's emphasis on praying to saints. 'I read Exodus 20:3–6,' she recalled, 'and suddenly I realized that it meant what it said. So I took all my statues of saints, put them in a carrier bag, left them in the church, and went off to find a church where the emphasis was on worshipping God alone.'

Proverbs 3:5–6

The Bible is central to guidance. But (with all respect to our friend at the top of the chapter) the idea is not to find a verse that justifies a specific course of action. Rather, it is to understand the text in its context, and to decide for ourselves what this means in terms of our lifestyles, as Ann did.

"The Bible doesn't name the person I should marry . . ."

Of course, the Bible doesn't tell me what church to go to, or what career to choose. It doesn't name the person I should marry, or tell me what kind of music I should listen to. It doesn't tell me what my specific gifts are, or whether I should live in Manchester or Peckham.

The Bible tells me what God is like. It tells me the kind of things that please him. It informs me very clearly about the actions and attitudes that God describes as sinful, and which I should thus avoid.

For instance, I might 'feel led' to fund missionary work out of the proceeds of robbing a bank. But the Bible says, 'Do not steal.' I might 'feel led' to marry Clare. But Clare is already married, and the Bible says a great deal about honouring marriage.

The Bible reveals God's will for all of us: his will that we find faith and new life in Jesus Christ; his will that we get involved with a local body of his people; his will that we share our faith with the people around us; his will that we show the reality of our faith by doing good works and loving our neighbour as ourselves.

2 Peter 3:9
James 2:26

A lot of our questions about guidance can be answered by reading, knowing and understanding Scripture. Is it God's will that I tell others that I'm a Christian? Read 1 Peter 3:16. Is it God's will that I attend church regularly? Read Hebrews 10:25. Is it God's will that I tell the truth at work? Read Colossians 3:9. Is it God's will that I forgive people who wrong me? Read Matthew 18:21–35. Is it God's will that I share what I have with those less fortunate than me? Read Titus 3:14.

For a whole raft of issues, we can find all the guidance we need by using a concordance or Bible dictionary that shows us where to look up what the Bible says about a particular topic.

But we also have to make decisions about a whole range of things the Bible doesn't speak about. Should I drive a car? Should I smoke? Should I be a lawyer, a manager, a journalist, a taxi-driver, a hairdresser, a brickie or a chippie? The Bible has nothing to say about

"God expects us to make wise decisions . . ."

these things, so it's no good opening it at random and hoping.

It is here that God expects us to make wise decisions based on our knowledge of him and of his Word, and on our conscious following of the Holy Spirit's promptings. Such guidance is not a matter of intuition or of 'feeling led', but of careful thought and prayer. And decisions arrived at by this process are open to scrutiny and question by others.

How does this approach to guidance work?

Who's pulling your strings?

'Well, there's a house with the job and you'll have a colleague,' Nick commented. It was not the answer I'd expected. Here I was on the verge of leaving college to go to my first pastorate, expecting some shaft of spiritual insight or pearl of wisdom, and all this lecturer can do is observe that there's a manse and someone to work with.

But there was method in his apparent madness. After all, what was I looking for? I had gone to college having decided that God wanted me to leave journalism and train for Christian ministry. Furthermore, I felt drawn by my experience and its needs to an inner-city area. I was a Baptist seeking accreditation by the Baptist Union, and this was a Baptist church.

'So I think you've landed on your feet. I couldn't take it. But it seems tailor-made for you,' he continued. 'Inner-city, good leadership, reasonable accommodation, a colleague. What does your wife think?'

'She's really keen.'

'Go for it. You won't get a better offer.'

Is that it? I thought. Shouldn't it be more spiritual – voices from heaven, verses leaping out at me from the pages of Deuteronomy, prophecies? Then Hugh's words came back to me. 'You make up your mind, you're growing up.'

The problem with guidance is that there are no hard and fast rules. It works slightly differently for everyone. But there are some general principles that we always have to keep in mind when making any decision. Of course, we normally speak of guidance only when we're considering a major decision such as choosing a career, changing a job, finding a marriage partner, or taking on major responsibility at church or in the community.

"It works slightly differently for everyone."

It's odd, but true, that we Christians don't seem overly concerned to seek guidance about how we use our money. Having put aside our 10% for Christian giving, we seem to assume that if we've got the money we can spend it on whatever takes our fancy. This is strange, because the Bible says a great deal about money – considerably more than it says about the gift of tongues or overseas missionary work. Yet few Christians seem to seek guidance from the Scriptures over their spending decisions.

E.g. *Luke 12:13–34*

*g*etting down to basics

The first principle is *'What does the Bible say?'* We've already said a good deal about that. Just to reiterate: God's Word contains a vast amount of practical wisdom about living and working in God's world. God has laid down laws and principles for the good ordering of our lives, and they should form the framework for all our thinking about life and work, family and church.

Psalm 119:105, 130

The second principle is summed up in the question *'What's happened so far?'* As he slept in the temple one night, Samuel was called by God to be a prophet. He was in the temple because of the choice his mother had made, and, no doubt, as he grew up, by his own choice. So, by the time God spoke to him that night, he already knew something about the Lord (not a great deal, judging by the speed of his response!).

1 Samuel 3:1–21

Similarly, we seek guidance, and hear God calling us to something new, when we're already in the middle of something. If I'm at university doing a degree in history, I am unlikely to consider a career in pharmacy. If I have no ability at learning foreign languages, despite the best efforts of school French and German teachers, I am unlikely to work in Christian ministry abroad. I say 'unlikely' in both those cases because God can do amazing things with unpromising material.

Put simply, the 'What's happened so far?' principle suggests that my life to date has suited me for certain things and not for others; that present choices are limited by past choices, and that there is no point pining for something that previous choices have rendered unlikely or impossible.

The third principle could be headed *'Does it make sense given all the circumstances?'* If I am seeking guidance about a job or a new role in the church, I need to ask certain searching questions. Can I do it? Do I want to do it? What effect will doing it have on other important parts of my life – family, friends, leisure, church, and so on?

If I am thinking of proposing to someone – a situation where rational thought is often furthest from our minds! – it is helpful to weigh up one or two issues. Is the person a Christian? Do I love him or her? Do we have anything in common? Does this person share my goals and ambitions? Do I share his or hers?

This last question is vital. When Linda and I were considering marriage, one of the factors we had to take account of was my sense of call to the Christian ministry. Did she share it? It would have been disastrous for us to marry with me keen to go into the ministry and Linda keen to talk me out of it. But it is amazing how many people go into marriage saying, 'I'll change him,' or 'She'll see it my way eventually.' Such marriages are rarely long-lasting, however 'led' the couple felt at the outset.

Fourthly, there's the *'What do others say?'* principle. We often hear God through what friends and family have to say about a course of action we are contemplating.

A group of people was discussing how they should move forward in evangelism. After a good hour of talking, someone said, rather piously, 'Well, let's seek the Lord's will about it, shall we?' (meaning, of course, 'Let's pray about it; we've talked long enough.')

Someone responded tartly: 'What do you think we've been doing for the past hour?' – the point being that talking over decisions we

". . . a situation where rational thought is often furthest from our minds . . ."

Proverbs 27:17

87

Acts 15:28

have to make is one way of finding out what God thinks. It's what the early church did when it had decisions to make. On one classic occasion, following much heated discussion, the apostles concluded: 'It has seemed good to the Holy Spirit and to us . . .'

Proverbs 27:6

When we are seeking guidance about personal decisions, it is good to talk them over with friends. Often they will ask questions we'd not thought of, expose motives we hadn't known were there, highlight effects the decision would have on us and on those around us that we hadn't foreseen. Of course, while talking things over with friends, we still have to make the decision for ourselves. Good friends will honour that decision, whether they agree with it or not.

The final principle is *the feel-good factor*. Having talked over the prospect of pastoring a church in Peckham with Nick, my lecturer, every time I thought about Peckham or the job I felt good. I felt a strange, nay irrational, warm glow – irrational, because if you know Peckham . . . (run-down inner-urban area, south of Westminster Bridge in London, for those of you unfortunate enough never to have been there!). Now I wouldn't trust my life to such feelings. And I certainly wouldn't put them above thinking and talking over decisions. I remember feeling good about the job Hugh had shot down in flames on excellent, rational grounds.

". . . he will give us the desire of our hearts . . ."

But the Bible says that if we commit our way to the Lord, he will give us the desire of our hearts. I remember talking to Colin about a role he'd been asked to take on in church. 'I think I ought to do it,' he told me. 'I think

God wants me to do it cos it'll be good for me.'

'Why's that?' I asked innocently.

'Because I really don't want to do it,' he said. 'I always think God gives us things we don't want.'

That is a tragic view of God and a disastrous view of guidance. Certainly, there are occasions when God calls us to take on something we don't feel qualified for, or for which we don't have a particular inclination. But to make that a principle of guidance is to condemn oneself to a life of unfulfilling drudgery.

Once we have committed our decision to God, the feel-good factor is one of those little confirmatory signs that God graciously gives us. Paul described it as 'the peace of God, which surpasses all understanding'.

Philippians 4:6–7

Guidance is a bit like riding a bike. You can balance on a bike only if you're moving (unless you're a circus performer!). Some of us stand still, rooted to the spot, vowing, 'I'm not moving until I get a word from the Lord.' But that's not the way it happens. God guides us as we're moving. We hear the voice saying, 'This way!' or 'That way!' as we are thinking, planning, living, walking on, following Jesus.

Isaiah 30:21

So get on your bike. Get on with your life. Make plans, take decisions, live. 'Keep in step with the Spirit' – that is to say, pay close attention to your relationship with the Lord – and he will ensure you don't go far wrong.

Galatians 5:25 (NIV)

*S*ome helpful books

There is a vast library of books on guidance. Apart from the Bible, the one I have found the most helpful is Garry Friesen, *Decision-making and the Will of God* (Multnomah). It is an excellent, liberating read. My one quibble with it is that Friesen makes the process of guidance a mite too rational, and seems to leave barely any room for God to surprise us.

Other helpful guides are Peter Adam, *Guidance* (Grove Spirituality series, 27, Grove Books) and Tom Sine's terrific *Why Settle for More and Miss the Best?* (Word).

On guidance about how we spend our money, Ronald Sider's *Rich Christians in an Age of Hunger* (Hodder and Stoughton, 1990 edition) is a must. Mike Starkey's *Born to Shop* (Monarch) is a riveting read, full of wry comment and helpful insights.

Robert Banks, *All the Business of Life* (Albatross), while not about guidance as such, is a very helpful look at bridging the gulf that exists between our 'spiritual' lives and our 'everyday working' lives.

WHATEVER HAPPENED TO THE WORLD AND THE FLESH?

6

There's a deep-rooted human tendency to pass the buck. Adam did it with Eve: 'The woman *you* gave me made me do it.' We hear it every day: 'It's not my fault; he made me do it.'

Christians aren't immune from this tendency. Being responsible for our actions can be very demanding, and if we can pass the buck to someone else, then we jump at the chance. 'I felt led to . . .' can sometimes be a way of making God responsible for all our decisions, good, bad and indifferent. And there's an increasing tendency to lay all the responsibility for our faults at the devil's door.

If we've had a bad day we protest, 'Satan's been on my back.' If we fall into sin we say, 'The devil led me astray.' If we're plagued by a nasty habit or by obsessive or compulsive behaviour we exclaim that we need deliverance. And there's no shortage of offers of help in that department.

There's a lot of talk about the devil and all his forces, but whatever happened to the world and the flesh?

*h*eavenly cowboys and Indians

One of the pictures the Bible uses to describe the Christian life is the powerful one of battle. It is not easy being the person God wants me to be. There are enemies trying to prevent me realizing my potential in Christ. So getting there is a struggle.

Christians have traditionally spoken of a threefold enemy: the world, the flesh and the devil. And in a day when Frank Peretti's lurid tales top the Christian bestseller lists, and every week a book on how to spot and zap demon activity is published, it's as well to remind ourselves what Scripture says about the three and how they are related.

'The world' in this context refers not to the physical creation which God loved so much that he redeemed it through the blood of his Son, but to the system of thinking and behaving that completely disregards God.

It is this that Paul is talking of when he warns the Colossians: 'See to it that no one takes you captive through philosophy and empty deceit, according to human tradition, according to the elemental spirits of the universe, and not according to Christ.' The phrase translated 'elemental spirits of the

"It is not easy being the person God wants me to be."

Colossians 2:8

92

universe' could be rendered 'the rudiments of the world'.

This is what James refers to when he says that 'friendship with the world is enmity with God', and what John is talking about when he says: 'Do not love the world or the things in the world; . . . for all that is in the world – the desire of the flesh, the desire of the eyes, the pride in riches – comes not from the Father but from the world.'

James 4:4
1 John 2:15–16

John's picture of the world is very helpful. 'The desire of the flesh' is doing what comes naturally, and what comes naturally to us is sin, as we'll see in a minute. 'The desire of the eyes' is the craving for what is seen. The world says that what you see is all there is, so live for that. The pride in riches speaks for itself. The world tells us to seek satisfaction in material things – be healthy, wealthy and wise, for life consists in the abundance of possessions – the very opposite of what Jesus says.

Luke 12:15

'The flesh' in this context refers to what dour old Christians in the circles I moved in as a young believer called 'the old man'. I thought they were referring to my father or their father. But in fact they meant our sinful human nature. It is what James was talking about when he said: 'One is tempted when, by his own evil desire, he is dragged away and enticed. Then, after desire has conceived, it gives birth to sin.'

James 1:14 (NIV)

It is what Paul is speaking of when he says: 'Live by the Spirit, I say, and do not gratify the desires of the flesh. For what the flesh desires is opposed to the Spirit, and what the Spirit desires is opposed to the flesh.' Elsewhere he speaks of the agony 'the flesh'

Galatians 5:16–17

causes the believer: 'For I do not do what I want, but I do the very thing I hate . . . For I know that nothing good dwells within me, that is, in my flesh. I can will what is right, but I cannot do it. For I do not do the good I want, but the evil I do not want is what I do.'

Romans 7:15, 18–19

The flesh is the 'me' that wants everything done to satisfy my needs, my whims, my wants. The flesh is the 'me' that is seeking an easy ride, with health and wealth and happiness all the way. The flesh wants to do it 'my way' and not God's. Not everything the flesh does is evil, or even wrong, in itself. But everything the flesh does is done without reference to God.

Paul lists the 'works of the flesh' just before the 'fruit of the Spirit' in Galatians. He says they are obvious, and so they are. Our problem when we read such a list is that we often assume it is talking about big sins and major faults – murder, adultery, bank heists and witchcraft – and so it is. But it is also talking about little faults, petty jealousies and quarrels, impure thoughts, dishonest and exaggerated stories, pride, envy of another Christian's gifts and abilities, unjustified anger. The list is unpleasant and seemingly endless.

Galatians 5:19–21

"The flesh is the 'me' that is seeking an easy ride . . ."

Paul's list also describes sins that we can all see in ourselves to one degree or another. This is not surprising. If we did *not* think and do such things, then surely Jesus would not have needed to go to the cross. The truth is that we are all like this, and only Jesus' death and resurrection can help us. 'Who will rescue me from this body of death? Thanks be to God through Christ Jesus our Lord!'

Romans 7:24–25

Ol' sticky fingers

The third member of this trinity of enemies is the devil. A venerable old saint was once asked to write a book on the doctrine of the devil. He thought about it for a while. His long experience in ministry had given him a good deal of understanding of the devil and all his works. But he firmly rejected the offer, telling his would-be publisher that 'the devil does not deserve a doctrine'. What a wise man!

The Bible tells us all we need to know about the devil in order to avoid being tangled up in his activities, but nothing further to satisfy our seemingly insatiable curiosity about him.

What the Bible clearly does not say is that Satan is the powerful ruler of a kingdom that is the equal and opposite of God's kingdom. The Bible does not picture a cold war between heaven and hell where two enemies, like the USA and USSR, armed to the teeth with enough weapons to ensure the other's destruction, struggle for possession of people's souls.

Stephen Gaukroger helpfully puts the devil in perspective. 'The Bible describes him as a cunning master of disguise with all the power of a roaring lion,' he says. 'Fortunately, he is a roaring lion on a chain. God is the all-powerful keeper of the zoo and will only allow him limited freedom. Not only this, by his Son's death and resurrection God has dealt this enemy of humanity a fatal blow. So he is a mortally wounded lion on a chain! . . . You have nothing to fear.'

This bucket of water certainly needs to be

DARE TO BREAK THE MOULD

". . . more from **Star Wars** *and* **Terminator 2** *than from the Bible . . ."*

Read Job 1 – 2

Colossians 2:15

James 4:7
Romans 16:19–20

poured on the overheated claims of those whose picture of spiritual warfare is derived more from *Star Wars* and *Terminator 2* than from the Bible. Of course, Stephen Gaukroger warns against a careless and carefree attitude towards the devil – even a caged wild animal is dangerous if you get too close – but his words are a timely reminder to us to keep a sense of proportion.

The devil's main weapon against us is our own sin. He accuses us before God of having sinned, of serving God only because it's to our advantage to do so, and of being a Christian only for what we can get out of it. So he marches into heaven and declaims: 'You know that Simon Jones? Well, I've just seen him eating too much cake, lusting after women and lying about his neighbours.' And if it were true, then God would have to agree, no doubt sadly, 'Yes, you're right; Simon's been sinning.'

The wonder of the gospel is that Satan's ground has been swept from beneath his feet. Jesus has triumphed over him totally on the cross, removing his right to accuse any Christian before God. So now, when Satan rolls into heaven and starts, 'You know that Simon Jones? . . .' God replies, 'Yes. He's forgiven. My Son died for him. He's clean. Get lost.'

Because we live under God's protection, we too can tell Satan to beat it. 'Submit yourselves therefore to God. Resist the devil, and he will flee from you,' says James. Paul agrees: 'I want you to be wise in what is good and guileless in what is evil. The God of peace will shortly crush Satan under your feet.' The message is: stay close to God, and the devil can't touch you.

The only ground Satan has for accusing me or any Christian is when we sin and don't confess it and repent of it. So he's looking for opportunities to trip us up. Peter says that he's like a roaring lion, seeking to devour people. The way he devours them is by tempting them to sin, leading them to fall, and then going to God and accusing them. He's like the kid in the school yard who dares you to climb the fence and then runs to teacher, yelling, 'Miss! Miss! Look, miss! He's up the fence . . .'

1 Peter 5:8

How does Satan tempt us? The Bible warns us that he is subtle and cunning. He rarely engages in full-frontal assault. He seldom shows his hand. He doesn't need to. He has two powerful allies: ourselves (the flesh) and the world we live in. So Scripture tells us little about combating Satan, and much about living good, wholesome, holy lives, keeping in step with the Spirit.

Read Genesis 3:1–13

As Charles Sherlock says: 'The struggle in which Christians are involved is not fundamentally negative (against evil) but positive, to do the will of God in a fallen creation.'

Charles Sherlock, *The Overcoming of Satan* (Grove Books), p. 4.

a fatal attraction

Many Christians are restless and dissatisfied with their lives. They feel they should be making more progress, but that they're being held back, and that something is preventing them from realizing their full potential in Christ. And too often they focus on that rather than on God.

Nigel Wright calls this 'a paranoid world-view'. Paranoia is the feeling that I'm always being followed, stared at, and scrutinized; that someone's out to get me. Paranoia makes us feel weak, insecure and vulnerable.

As we saw in our chapter on worship, what we focus our attention on assumes ever greater significance in our lives. If it is God, then he is magnified, made larger, in our conscious minds. If it is the devil and all his forces, then the unfortunate consequence is that we are constantly looking over our shoulder, fearfully wondering when his next attack will come, unable to move on in our faith.

'I need counselling,' announced Brian, a bright, gifted, outgoing young man, hugging his knees in the corner of my study.

'What for?' I enquired.

'I'm not sure really. I just know that something is wrong and I need to get it out of my life before I can get anywhere.'

I pressed him further. 'What areas of your life does this affect?'

'All of it,' he said.

We met again a few days later. He was worse. 'I went to a meeting where people prayed for me and told me I'd been delivered of a demon,' he told me. 'How can I be so evil that I was possessed? I really need help now.'

I probed for details of what happened at the meeting. I firmly believe in the demonic. I also firmly believe that much harm is done by expelling demons that aren't there. There is a dangerous tendency among evangelicals today to equate experience with truth and reality.

When I sit on a cliff overlooking the sea

". . . expelling demons that aren't there . . ."

98

watching a sunset, what I see isn't happening. I see the sun sinking below the horizon. But I know in my head that the sun isn't moving. I know that the Earth is moving but I can neither see nor feel it. I know, because of what I've read about the nature of the universe, that the Earth revolves around the sun, whatever my eyes tell me.

It is the same with the Christian life. 'Experience must always give way to revelation,' says Selwyn Hughes. 'The final referee in everything must be the Bible.'

My friend Brian's very real experience could be interpreted in a number of ways. But that wasn't really his problem. As we talked it became clear that at the heart of his confusion lay a misunderstanding of what the Bible says about people, the threefold enemy we face, and the resources available to us to help us live wholesome Christian lives.

*t*o boldly go

The Christian life is a battle. As we have seen, it is not first and foremost a battle against the devil and the forces of evil. Rather, it is a battle to do the will of God, to keep the faith. As Paul said to Timothy shortly before his martyrdom: 'I have fought the good fight, I have finished the race, I have kept the faith.'

2 Timothy 4:7

How can we ensure that we do the same?

The first thing we need to do is to *be sure whom we fear*. The paranoid worldview sees the devil as someone to fear. The Bible says we shouldn't. Of course we should be wary of him; we should not flirt with him or be flippant about him and his tactics. But fear is reserved for God.

Jesus tells us: 'Do not fear those who kill the body, and after that can do nothing more. But I will warn you whom to fear: fear him who, after he has killed, has authority to cast into hell. Yes, I tell you, fear him!' Peter says bluntly, 'Fear God.'

Luke 12:4–5
1 Peter 2:17

The fear of the Lord is not a cringing terror of God. It is reverent awe. It is recognizing that God is all-powerful and beyond our comprehension, and responding to him in the only way appropriate: humble submission. That's why Peter urges us to 'humble [ourselves] therefore under the mighty hand of God'.

1 Peter 5:6

Those who fear God put themselves in a position to know his peace, his protection from harm, his provision for our needs, and his power to win through. Fear of the Lord concentrates our minds on being pure before him above everything else. And those who fear God give him pleasure. Truly, if we fear God, we need fear nothing and no-one else.

Psalms 34:6–10; 147:11

Secondly, we are to *follow God*. The Christian life is a journey and Jesus is the way. Following God therefore means doing the sort of things that Jesus did, living the kind of life he lived, and being like him. Paul sums this up in these words: 'I want to know Christ and the power of his resurrection and the sharing of his sufferings by becoming like him in his death.' Being like Jesus involves both glory and death, pain and ecstasy, wonderful joy and deep sorrow. Compared to knowing Jesus, says Paul, everything else is junk.

John 14:6
Ephesians 5:1
Philippians 3:10

". . . everything else is junk . . ."

Thirdly, keeping the faith is a *fight*. We

struggle against pressure from the world to conform to its ways. We battle with our own desires to sin, to do things our way, and to satisfy the longings of our old nature. We fight to do the will of God, to follow him, to please him, and to serve him. And as we do that, we are rejecting the devil's agenda for our lives. As we stick close to God and God's way for us, resisting any alternatives, so the devil can gain no foothold in our lives, no ground for accusation before God.

*m*aking the right choice

The fight is focused on our lifestyle. The New Testament frequently tells us to 'get rid of' certain kinds of behaviour as if they were filthy old garments, and to be 'clothed' with other kinds. The stress is on the fact that it is something *we* do; God doesn't do it to us. And we don't do it just once. We do it every day. Peter calls us 'to live for the rest of [our] earthly life no longer by human desires but by the will of God'. He says we've spent enough time sinning; it is time to choose to do things God's way.

Colossians 3:8–10
1 Peter 4:2–4

Paul has a similar message when he tells the Ephesians, 'You were taught to put away your former way of life, your old self, corrupt and deluded by its lusts, and to be renewed in the spirit of your minds, and to clothe yourselves with the new self, created according to the likeness of God in true righteousness and holiness.' He goes on to spell out how this happens as we choose to do what God approves of, and to turn our backs on the ways of the world.

Ephesians 4:22–24

Ephesians 4:26–27

For instance, Paul warns them not to let their anger simmer away, because that gives the devil a foothold. The same probably applies to other areas of behaviour: as we do things our way rather than God's, it gives the devil ground for accusation against us.

Ephesians 6:18–20

We are not alone or weaponless in our fight. The key weapon we have is prayer, the prayer that cries out to God for strength and aid in the thick of the battle – as Jesus did. I hear Christians 'coming against the evil one' and 'binding him in Jesus' name'. This seems a curiously negative way of praying and one that is possibly motivated more by fear of the devil than by faith in God. It is surely better to pray, 'Your will be done, . . . lead us not into temptation, but deliver us from the evil one', as Jesus taught us to.

Matthew 6:9–13 (NIV)

As a young Christian I was told to keep short accounts with God. A wise old Christian said to me, 'When you fall – and you will – don't wallow. Get up. Get cleaned off. Get on with living.' Let's confess our sins to God in the sure and certain knowledge that he'll forgive us. Then let's get up and move on with him.

1 John 1:8–10

"To win the battle with the flesh we will need to starve the old life and feed the new."
Stephen Gaukroger

Ephesians 4:17–24; 5:15–17; 6:17
Romans 12:1–2

Our other weapon is the Bible, 'the sword of the Spirit'. This tells us what God approves of and what he calls sin. It is vital for the renewing of our minds (which Paul speaks of in Ephesians and Romans) that we read and get to know Scripture. For Paul, obedience starts in the mind, that is, what we think about. Our minds need to be marinated in Scripture so that over time we grow to think the way its Author does.

Finally, we need to *remember that we aren't alone* in the battle. We live in fellowship with other Christians. The armour Paul talks of in Ephesians 6 is best worn in company with others. His description is drawn from the Roman soldiers he saw about him all the time. One of the secrets of the Roman legions' strength was the support the soldiers gave each other. Their shields locked together to form an impregnable shell known as a 'tortoise', which protected the whole troop from incoming arrows and opponents' swords.

We need to pray for one another; to encourage, teach, support, forgive and otherwise help one another. That is what the church is for. Isolated warriors stand very little chance on the battlefield. Together, however, an army has the strength to stand and advance according to its leader's orders.

Colossians 3:12–16

Of course, we don't have fellowship only with one another. We also have fellowship with God. Paul reminds the Philippians that 'it is God who is at work in you, enabling you both to will and to work for his good pleasure'. He had already assured them that 'the one who began a good work among you will bring it to completion by the day of Jesus Christ'.

Philippians 2:13; 1:6

Not only is God working in and among us in a general way to give us the strength to do his will; he also comes alongside us at the very time when we need his presence specifically to resist sin and to choose his way. Writing to the Thessalonians, urging them to resist sexual temptation, Paul assures them that it is right in the thick of the battle, just when the temptation is at its most acute, that God gives us his Holy Spirit.

1 Thessalonians 4:3–8

"Life is not a problem to be solved but a work to be made."

We're getting there

Dorothy L. Sayers once said that 'life is not a problem to be solved but a work to be made.' There is no shortcut to holiness. We cannot be delivered to a higher plane where the temptations common to men and women no longer affect us.

Life is a struggle: the struggle of the artist to create a Venus de Milo from a lump of rock; the struggle of the gardener to turn a wilderness into ordered beauty; the struggle of the poet to form a jumble of ideas into *King Lear*.

The struggle is both ours (as we seek to resist the pull of the world, to control the desires of our flesh, and to do the will of our Father) and God's (as he seeks to work in our lives by his Spirit).

The great comfort and encouragement is that the power behind the work is all God's. We are the lump of rock, the barren wilderness, the jumble of fragments that God turns into a masterpiece. Whatever the world, the flesh and the devil try to do, as we keep in step with God, his purpose for us cannot be thwarted.

a little light reading

There's a lot of stuff available on the devil and demons and detailed strategies for spiritual warfare that's best left on the shelves.

By far the most helpful book I've come across is Charles Sherlock's booklet *The Overcoming of Satan* (Grove Spirituality series, 17, Grove Books). Also good is Nigel Wright,

The Fair Face of Evil (Marshall Pickering), and Clinton Arnold, *Powers of Darkness* (IVP) – though his more technical study, *Ephesians: Power and Magic* (Baker Book House) is better if you've the stamina.

Walter Wink, *Naming the Powers* (Marshall Pickering), is a fascinating study of the whole concept of power – both spiritual and secular – in the New Testament. As I write this, Selwyn Hughes is producing a most helpful series of articles entitled 'The Demonic in Counselling' in the journal *The Christian Counsellor* (starting in volume 2, number 1), which I have quoted in this chapter. The Stephen Gaukroger quotations came from *Making it Work* (SU), which has a very good chapter on enemies.

And, of course, C. S. Lewis, *The Screwtape Letters*, is still essential reading.

I'm grateful to Philip Yancey for the Dorothy L. Sayers quotation.

TAKING CHARGE

A recent British Gas television advertising campaign aimed to stress the convenience and controllability of gas. It featured famous actors and movie stars who produced a flame by snapping their fingers. Thumb ablaze, they exclaimed, 'Don't you just love being in control?'

Sadly, too many Christians want to hand over control to someone else. And it isn't God. Michael Saward spoke recently about there being a 'Führer mentality' among some Christians – a desire to have other people make all the decisions about what we'll believe and how we'll behave.

Jesus, just like British Gas, wants to put us

Galatians 5:23

". . . he hands back control of our lives to us . . ."

in control. Hence the fruit of the Holy Spirit. The last one mentioned in the list in Galatians (and for that reason possibly the one that underpins and makes possible the other eight) is self-control.

This is an amazing fact if we'd only step back to think about it. The Lord of glory has rescued us from sin and death, and from domination by the world, the flesh and the devil, because we could not do it ourselves. And having done that, he hands back control of our lives to us. The fruit of the Spirit is not God-control – 'Jesus wants me for a robot' should not be sung in our churches. The fruit of the Spirit is *self*-control.

The apostle Paul sets great store by self-control. The late great F. F. Bruce called him 'the apostle of the free spirit'. Another leading scholar, Richard Longenecker, called him 'the apostle of liberty'. For Paul, self-control is a vital part of Christian freedom, of being the person God intends us to be, and of living the life God intends us to live.

In his discussion on freedom in 1 Corinthians 8, 9 and 10, Paul compares Christians to athletes who exercise self-control in order to win the prize. He speaks of his determination not to be dominated by anything or anyone, and of not allowing anything to manipulate or control him other than his desire to do the will of God.

Writing to Titus with instructions about what this young minister in his team should do on Crete, Paul outlines what should be taught in church. And it all boils down to self-control. 'Tell the older men to be . . . self-controlled . . . The young women . . . to be self-controlled . . . Similarly, encourage

Titus 2:2, 4–6 (NIV)

the young men to be self-controlled.'

For Paul, self-control was fundamental. It was about keeping in step with the Spirit and doing God's will. What Paul wanted to see around the Mediterranean world of his day was not a host of Paul-clones, all doing and saying exactly the same things that he did. Although he probably knew that you're never alone with a clone, he also knew that God had made people richly and wonderfully different, endowed them with a wide variety of gifts and talents, life stories and ways of responding to him, and set them free to live the life God intended for them.

". . . a cabbage or any other vegetable . . ."

Self-control is about taking charge. Jesus doesn't want me for a cabbage or any other vegetable. Jesus wants me as a free member of his multicoloured body on earth. On the cross he washed away the dark, drab grey of conformity to sin and opened up a whole spectrum of possibilities for those who put their trust in him.

The wonder of the Christian life is that Jesus frees us from sin, from the world's mould, from the flesh and from the devil, in order that we may find freedom in the amazing world of his salvation.

There are as many ways of being a biblical Christian as there are biblical Christians in the world. Take control of your life. Don't let the world or the church or the latest Christian fad squeeze you into its mould. Then take Jesus' hand and launch out into the adventure of faith. Dare to break the mould.

ACKNOWLEDGMENTS

We gratefully acknowledge permission to quote from the following copyright material:

Page 45
'World of Wonders' on the album of the same name. Written by Bruce Cockburn. Published by Golden Mountain Music – administered by Bugle Songs Ltd © 1985. Published by kind permission.

'Somebody Touched Me' on the album *Nothing But a Burning Light*. Written by Bruce Cockburn. Published by Golden Mountain Music – administered by Bugle Songs Ltd © 1991. Published by kind permission.

'When I Look to the Mountains' on the album *Celebrate this Heartbeat* by Randy Stonehill. Copyright © Stonehillian Music/ Word Music/Word Music (UK). Administered by CopyCare Ltd, 8 Marshfoot Lane, Hailsham, East Sussex BN27 2RA, UK. Used by permission.

Page 58
The quotation from Joni Mitchell's song 'In France They Kiss on Main Street', on the album *The Hissing of Summer Lawns*, is reproduced by permission of Warner Chappell Music Ltd./International Music Publications.